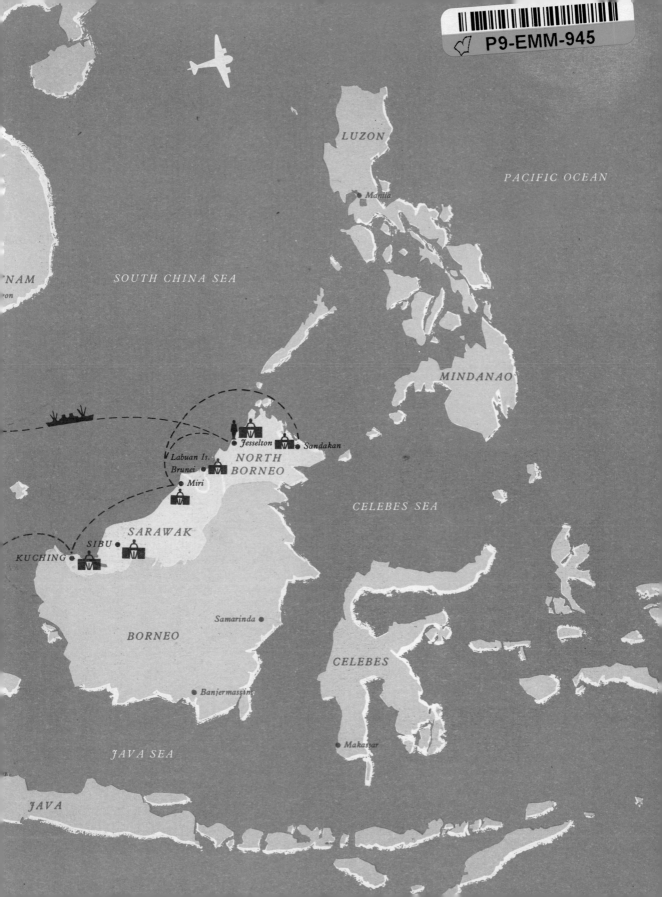

LUZON

PACIFIC OCEAN

Manila

SOUTH CHINA SEA

'NAM

MINDANAO

Jesselton

Sandakan

Labuan Is.
Brunei

NORTH
BORNEO

Miri

CELEBES SEA

SARAWAK

SIBU

KUCHING

BORNEO

Samarinda

CELEBES

Banjermassim

JAVA SEA

Makassar

JAVA

# THE BORNEO STORY

*James Brooke, founder of Sarawak, and the first 'White Rajah'*

# The
# BORNEO STORY

## THE HISTORY OF THE FIRST 100 YEARS
## OF TRADING IN THE FAR EAST BY
## THE BORNEO COMPANY LIMITED

## *by Henry Longhurst*

*NEWMAN NEAME LIMITED*
*LONDON*

*First published in* 1956
*by* NEWMAN NEAME LIMITED
50 Fitzroy Street, London W1

*for* The BORNEO COMPANY LIMITED
143 Fenchurch Street, London EC3

*Printed in Great Britain*
*by* Percy Lund, Humphries & Co. Ltd,
London and Bradford
ALL RIGHTS RESERVED

# AUTHOR'S FOREWORD

*A writer is by no means averse to having hard work done on his behalf by someone else. In this connection I should like to express profound gratitude to Miss Margaret MacKay and Mr Charles Martine. Miss MacKay joined the Borneo Company an unstated number of years ago as a girl in pigtails, and service to the Company, in what may be called its human relationships with the staff, has been her life work. Her countless hours of research into its past have been, I believe, a labour of love. Mr Martine, now in the London office, joined the Company in Singapore in 1921 and at the outbreak of war was manager in Sarawak (which, for those not familiar with that part of the world, is pronounced 'Sarārw'k'). During his long internment by the Japanese in Changi Gaol he made pencilled notes of the Company's background, and these, together with his personal help, have been invaluable.*

*All of us are grateful to Miss Heather Harvey, granddaughter of the first managing director, and Miss Estelle Gardner, granddaughter of Ludvig Helms, for their help in delving into the past; and to His Serene Highness the Thai Ambassador – whose indulgence we ask for referring to his country by its more common usage in English-speaking countries, Siam – for the picture of King Chulalongkorn.*

H.L.

*His Highness Sir Charles Vyner Brooke, GCMG, Rajah of Sarawak*

# FOREWORD

BY HIS HIGHNESS THE RAJAH OF SARAWAK
SIR CHARLES VYNER BROOKE, GCMG

*I am pleased to have been given the opportunity of writing a foreword to this book, which has been produced to mark the completion of one hundred years' trading in the Far East by The Borneo Company Limited.*

*As the name of the Company denotes, one of the primary objects behind its formation in 1856 was to assist in developing the natural resources and the trade of Sarawak – an object dear to the heart of my ancestor, the first Rajah, and to his successors. So strong was the link between the State of Sarawak and the Borneo Company in the very early days that Sarawak and the Borneo Company were almost synonymous terms.*

*The Company's activities naturally extended to other territories in the Far East – to Siam, the Malayan Peninsula, and to what is now known as Indonesia, in which areas additional opportunities offered themselves. I feel, however, that it is nowadays very little realised what a tremendous help and support the Borneo Company was when Sarawak was fighting its way into existence; and I would add that the present-day progress and prosperity of the Country can be clearly traced to the great efforts of this Company in those early days when capital outlay and unremitting labour reaped no spectacular reward.*

*No doubt the major expansion of the Company's trading and organisation has taken place during the past twenty-five years, despite the temporary but crippling effect of nearly four years' occupation by the Japanese of all territories within the scope of its operations.*

*But the story which follows may well surprise and will undoubtedly interest many, and I feel confident that as the Company embarks upon its second century of progress it will do so with enthusiasm coupled with the same regard for human values and service as it has invariably shown in the past. May the Borneo Company continue to prosper.*

C. V. Brooke.
Rajah of Sarawak

# THE BORNEO COMPANY

Though its influence as one of the great British trading concerns of the East spreads over the whole of what we now call South East Asia, and though its first headquarters were in Singapore, there is only one place in which to open the story of the Borneo Company, and that is Borneo. No man living today can tell us what Borneo was like a hundred years ago. Maps bore no relation to fact, and it is fair to assume that throughout the first fifty years of the Company's existence the average Englishman's knowledge of that vast island was limited to a single expression – the Wild Men of Borneo.

Fortunately, however, there remains the evidence of one man who reveals not only what Borneo was like but what it was like to get there. As he reads it, the first-class traveller of today, wafted through the skies in his pressurised cabin and pausing comfortably between the sheets at successive night stops, may lift his hat and be thankful.

Ludvig Verner Helms was a Dane. Long to be associated with the Borneo Company, though he did not know it at the time, he left his native land in September 1846, in the brig *Johanna Caesar*, bound for the island of Bali, amid whose primitive and exotic beauty a fellow countryman was said to be the only white man yet to establish himself. Forty years later, when his wanderings had taken him not only to Bali but to Borneo, Siam, China, Japan, Australia and California, he told his story in a book *Pioneering in the Far East*. His voyage to Singapore will have been similar to that of the founders of the Borneo Company and some indeed may have sailed in the same convoy.

It took him seven days to reach the white cliffs of Dover. The *Johanna Caesar* found the convoy, eighty-five ships in all, lying in the Downs off Deal, within a mile or so of the present Royal Cinque Ports golf links – a scene so graphically recorded by William Hickey, the diarist – and together they beat down Channel, narrowly escaping collision during the night. Four days saw them off Bordeaux, when a gale drove them back on their course.

*Ludvig Verner Helms before leaving his native Denmark for the Far East in 1846. Helms spent twenty years in the Company's service, helping to create the modern state of Sarawak*

The hatches were battened down and the man at the helm was lashed securely to the wheel 'where, amidst the wildest tossings, he might comfortably assure himself that, if the ship went to the bottom, he would still be at his post.' The nine passengers were stowed away in the cabin below – 'a pestiferous hole with nothing to cheer us except the reflection that, as no attempt was made to cook any food, it was perhaps fortunate that we were too ill to eat it, and with no excitement beyond the unpleasant one of hearing that a sailor had been washed overboard.'

On 4th December, more than two months later, they began to look out for the Cape, but the captain had miscalculated the position and they did not reach it till the 14th – a difference which alone would enable a member of the Company today to fly from London to Borneo, transact some business and be back in Fenchurch Street. After a short stop at the Cape, during which a 72-year-old Baptist minister with whom he had been sharing a cabin invited him to assist in smuggling ashore a vast quantity of jewellery and gold watches, Helms continued his journey, frequently becalmed, once landing on some uninhabited tropical paradise only to be eaten alive by mosquitoes and nearly by an alligator, and on the last day of February – having started in September – he arrived at Singapore, an imposing looking town with esplanades, gardens, churches, public buildings and inviting looking villas, 'one of the finest of the many watch-towers which Britain, for political or commercial reasons, has placed about the earth.'

At this point we may pause to introduce the Brooke family, the 'White Rajahs' of Sarawak, whose dynasty was so intimately intertwined with the Borneo Company and whose story is unparalleled in the annals of British colonial enterprise.

James Brooke, soldier, traveller, and one time servant of the East India Company, was born at Bath in 1803. At the age of twenty-two, while serving in Burma, he was badly wounded in action and sent home by the Company with five years' leave of absence and a life pension of seventy pounds. He was shipwrecked on his way back to India in 1830, and proceeded to Madras in the *Castle of Huntly*, a slow vessel which successfully prevented his reaching Calcutta before the expiry of his time with the Company. The *Castle of Huntly* was going on to China and with it went Brooke. The voyage gave him his first sight of the islands of the East, and eventually decided the pattern of his remarkable life. He fell completely

*Left: Helms' clerk and factotum, 'my faithful Abdullah who for twenty years served the Company with unsurpassed devotion'; and, right, Helms towards the close of a singularly adventurous life. He died in Hampstead, aged ninety-three*

under their spell. He was captivated by their beauty, their remoteness, their primitive savagery, and the veil of mystery with which in those days they were still enshrouded. One day he would return, explore, and, who knows, rescue some small potential paradise from barbarism and make it his own. He was the victim of an urge which has moved the British since first they learnt to sail the sea in ships.

Brooke's chance came eight years later when his father died and left him a sizable fortune. He re-equipped the 140-ton schooner *Royalist*, and in 1838, eight years before Helms, sailed on his great adventure.

At this time, the island of Borneo was virtually unknown even in Singapore. The Sultan of Brunei was known only by name, and his sovereignty was assumed to cover the whole north-west coast. The province of Sarawak was ostensibly governed by the Sultan's uncle, Muda Hassim, but what with headhunting, tribal warfare, and universal corruption on the grand scale, the word 'government' was perhaps an optimistic description of his activities. However, at the time of Brooke's arrival in Singapore some ship-wrecked sailors brought accounts of kindly treatment at the hands of Muda Hassim and, the Singapore authorities wishing to make some acknowledgment of this kindly act, Brooke accepted a commission to take letters and presents across to Sarawak. He anchored at Kuching on 15th August, 1839, and at first sight decided that this was the object of his dreams. He determined to stay there and on that day the history of modern Sarawak may be said to have begun.

It was, as Helms later recorded, 'a strange determination for an English gentleman of independent fortune, eminently suited to enjoy social life and aspire to worldly distinction, of his own free will to choose a scene like this for his life's labour – for what was Sarawak at this time? A few scattered communities still remained on the most inaccessible parts of the limestone hills, which stand out like islands from the level sea jungle. These poor emaciated Dyaks passed a wretched existence amidst pigs and filth, living in continual dread, at times descending into the lower valleys in search of food, but furtively, as the timid deer, lest the stronger hostile tribes be upon them.'

*Helms' first office and bungalow beside the river at Kuching*

PROFIT & LOSS ACCOUNT – 31ST OCTOBER 1857

CREDIT

| | | | |
|---|---|---|---|
| By profit realised on specie sold in Calcutta | 728 | 8 | 7 |
| By profit realised on sundry parcels sago & sago flour | 2630 | 8 | 0 |
| By profit realised on vegetable tallow *Ann* | 12 | 8 | 11 |
| By profit realised on vegetable tallow sago *Sonora* | 8 | 16 | 7 |
| By profit realised on vegetable tallow sago *Heathpark* | 69 | 0 | 9 |
| By profit realised on vegetable tallow sago *Caroline Agnes* | 44 | 6 | 10 |
| Amount of dividend on shares taken back by the Company and debited this a/c on 1st May | 217 | 10 | 0 |
| By profit realised on various parcels of antimony crude & ore      11935 . 7 . 4 | | | |
| Less Royalty paid to Sir James Brooke for which antimony has yet to arrive    3570 . 5 . 0 | 8365 | 2 | 4 |
| | 12076 | 2 | 0 |
| Profit to credit of account on 31st October 1857 | 362 | 2 | 10 |

## PROFIT AND LOSS ACCOUNT – 31ST OCTOBER 1857

DEBIT

| | | | | |
|---|---|---|---|---|
| To dividend etc paid to shareholders & directors | | 5773 | 15 | 3 |

**Sarawak Riots**

| | | | | |
|---|---|---|---|---|
| Amount of cash stolen during riots | $6359 . 79 | | | |
| Wages to sago coolies during time factory was closed | 885 . 08 | | | |
| Wages various servants ditto | 304 . 97 | | | |
| Wages ore workers | 237 . 43 | | | |
| Mr. Helms' expenses to Serebas | 126 . 82 | | | |
| Cost of various tools stolen | 13 . 68 | | | |
| | 7927 . 77 | | | |
| Less amount recovered | 200 . 00 | | | |
| $7727 . 77 @ 5/– | | 1931 | 18 | 10 |
| To loss on gutta percha sold in Singapore | | 45 | 1 | 1 |
| To amount of office expenses, clerks salaries, law expenses, books, stationery, office furniture, seals, bill forms and various other expenses etc. connected with home and abroad | | 1594 | 17 | 0 |

Amount of interest paid to

| | | | | |
|---|---|---|---|---|
| shareholders | 1498 .17 . 2 | | | |
| sundry accts. | 371 . 9 . 9 | | | |
| | 1861 . 6 .11 | | | |
| Less amount of interest recd. from sundry accts. | 457 .16 . 8 | 1403 | 10 | 04 |
| To freight paid in Singapore to vessels chartered to carry various cargoes from Sarawak to Singapore in transit to England | | 964 | 16 | 9 |
| | | 11713 | 19 | 2 |

The population immediately surrounding the humble bungalow which Brooke erected for himself consisted mainly of corrupt Malays 'divided broadly speaking into two classes, *viz.* nobles and slaves, poor and idle.' 'What a task,' Helms went on, 'for unaided private enterprise! To stop and turn back the savagery and decay of centuries, to step in between the oppressor and oppressed with a code of morals and ideas of justice hardly comprehensible to them; to brave all the perils of open enmity and secret treachery and of warlike expeditions in feverish jungles, with the anxieties of pecuniary deficiencies for the wants of government' – to say nothing of people at home, headed by Joseph Hume and others in Parliament, who soon presumed to sit in judgment, as they so often do today, on their own countrymen reaching out to bring the hand of civilisation to remote quarters of the globe.

In 1841, when Brooke had been there two years, there occurred what is generally described as a rebellion – it was probably an unusually savage outbreak of the normal condition of assorted raids and riots rather than a rebellion against established authority – and for his part in restoring order, Brooke, who with the aid of Admiral Sir Henry Keppel had already suppressed some of the more flagrant forms of piracy, was made Rajah of Sarawak by the Sultan of Brunei. There seems little doubt that he was acclaimed with enthusiasm by all but the most lawless elements of the population, and no doubt whatever that he and his successors, together with the Borneo Company, 'made' Sarawak.

Though we shall, of course, hear more of them later, it may be convenient here to summarise their story. In 1863 James Brooke was recognised by the British Government, having been knighted in 1848. He died in 1868 and was succeeded by his nephew, Sir Charles Johnson Brooke, who in 1870 concluded a treaty with Her Majesty's Government whereby Britain would deal on Sarawak's behalf with foreign states, but the internal administration of the State would rest entirely with the Rajah – thus conferring on Sarawak and the Brooke family a status unique in the history of the British Empire. Sir Charles was succeeded in 1917 by his son Sir Charles Vyner Brooke, writer of the foreword of this story, who ruled over Sarawak for twenty-nine years till its cession to the British Government in 1946.

*    *    *

In the middle 1850s Singapore, which had been ceded initially as wasteland to Sir Stamford Raffles on behalf of the East India Company in 1819, was only thirty years old. The great trading firms destined to become household names throughout the East were born from small syndicates of what may in the best sense be termed merchant adventurers – a great proportion of them, as would have been found in trading outposts all over the world in that age of expansion, being Scotsmen. Though glorified by the addition of 'and Company', a firm would consist perhaps of the head of the syndicate, his second-in-command, and two or three young European assistants as 'clerks'. As new opportunities for individual enterprise unfolded, the clerks tended to branch off on their own, generally with the blessing and often with the private assistance of their principals. Everything was new and there was room for all.

The firm of W. R. Paterson and Company was typical. In 1846 they had two partners, Paterson and William Morgan, in Glasgow, and managers in Manila, Batavia and Singapore. The manager in Singapore was Robert MacEwen from the west coast of Scotland, and one of his clerks was John Harvey, who came from Renfrewshire. Paterson retired in 1849, and the firm became MacEwen and Company, with Morgan and MacEwen in Glasgow, John Harvey now elevated to be manager in Singapore, and his younger brother Robert Harvey as one of the clerks.

By this time Brooke had been Rajah of Sarawak for the best part of ten years and the fruits of his labours were becoming evident in Singapore. Kuching was a free port; there was apparently settled government; there was certainly antimony, gold and coal; what else might be developed, given the money, remained to be seen. To MacEwen and Company, and especially to John Harvey, their managing director on the spot, it seemed an admirable prospect.

The Borneo Company, of 25 Mincing Lane, was registered in London in June 1856, and as such celebrates its centenary this year. It would not be fair to say either that MacEwens formed it on their own or that it was formed independently and then swallowed up MacEwens. Let us say that it was a case of six of one and half a dozen of the other. At any rate, the Company set up with a capital of £60,000 – today it is £2,000,000 – and the first board of directors were Robert Henderson, of R. & J. Henderson, Merchants, of Glasgow and London (Chairman); John Charles Templer, a lifelong friend of the Rajah (Vice-Chairman); James Dyce Nicol; John

Smith; Francis Richardson, a MacEwen partner and one time manager in Manila; and John Harvey, who was to remain managing director in the East.

The Rajah gave them far reaching development rights under a royalty arrangement with the Sarawak Treasury – among other things to 'take over and work Mines, Ores, Veins or Seams of all descriptions of Minerals in the Island of Borneo, and to barter or sell the produce of such workings.' They already had interests in other parts of the world, some of them inherited through MacEwens – and a fortunate thing it was to prove at that – but the very name of the Company shows the direction in which their eyes were mainly turned a hundred years ago.

If Brooke, the Borneo Company, and, as I am sure he would like it to be felt, Helms, 'made' Sarawak, the raw material from which they made it was raw indeed, even if at first sight it may at times have seemed very heaven. Helms could well understand, he said, how the first glimpse of Borneo may have inspired a romantic disposition, with picturesque mountains

*'A man never knew when all that would be left of him would be his head, baked, shrivelled and suspended with others from a pole like so many Spanish onions . . .'*

*The path of the pioneers; prospecting in Upper Sarawak in the 1870s*

rising 5,000 feet from the sea and a succession of foothills and river valleys stretching down to a sea-shore bordered by casuarinas or mangrove trees. What is more, the climate, though the rainfall at Kuching is 160 inches a year, proved ideal for Europeans.

Closer experience, however, revealed a different picture. The lowlands were a jungle swamp full of snakes, crocodiles, and insects bearing diseases known and unknown. The primitive inhabitants were riddled with smallpox (James Brooke contracted it in 1853 and, though he recovered, was never the same man again). Tribal warfare and headhunting were indiscriminate and incessant. A man never knew when within a few days all that would be left of him might be his head, baked, shrivelled, and suspended with others from a pole, like so many Spanish onions. Alternatively, if he put out to sea, he was liable to be intercepted and slaughtered by the piratical Sea Dyaks.

This was the scene over which James Brooke had been acclaimed Rajah in 1841. The progress he made, at first almost singlehanded, in reducing this barbarous outpost to some semblance of civilisation is almost incredible. When Helms arrived ten years later in the steamship *Pluto* from Singapore, as agent of an unnamed commercial firm, 'to buy up the antimonial ore and generally to develop the trade of the country,' he found a comfortable Government House in process of construction, half a dozen European bungalows and a pretty little church. The Rajah being on a visit to England, Helms was greeted by his nephew, Captain Brooke (who did not in fact, through an unhappy dispute, succeed him) and was made welcome to stay in Government House. Later in the day he was introduced to Mr Arthur Crookshank, the magistrate; Mr Ruppell, Treasurer; Mr Spencer St John, the Rajah's secretary; Mr Crymble, in charge of the fort; the missionaries, Fox, Nicholls, and Chambers; and Mr Hentig, a planter.

A month later he took possession of his own little mat-bungalow, a square box of palm leaves divided into bedroom and sitting room with a verandah overlooking the town and the river, his staff consisting of a Chinese cook and a Kling clerk and factotum, 'my faithful Abdullah who for twenty years served the Company and myself with unsurpassed devotion.' Abdullah was his only assistant then and their business transactions were trifling, but 'thousands of men,' he adds grandly, 'were to work for us, directly or indirectly, before I left.'

The bungalow was in a small clearing surrounded by sombre forest and neither of the two servants 'lived in', yet Helms was able to sleep alone in peaceful security and later to look back on his first five years in Sarawak – before disaster, sudden and complete, stole down in the night upon him, the Rajah, and the Borneo Company – as 'a period of uneventful quiet, to be looked upon with unfeigned pleasure.'

Helms' daily life at this time was full of a stimulating variety, spiced with danger, and is of interest because it must reflect exactly the sort of life led by the succession of young fellows who entered the Company's service and spent the next thirty or forty years building up the prosperity of Sarawak. His main business was to attend to the working and shipping of the antimony ore*, which was obtained by Chinese and Malay gold-diggers, together with land- and sea-Dyaks now working in comparative harmony under the beneficent influence of Brooke. The men worked in small scattered parties, mainly in the country between the two streams of the

*Antimony is a bluish white, exceedingly brittle metal, valuable medicinally and as an alloy. It acts like arsenic as an emetic, slows the heart and lowers the temperature. It is used as an alloy with lead in ammunition, and with tin to form type-metal. Indeed the type used in the printing of this book may conceivably contain antimony from mines opened up by the Borneo Company a hundred years ago.

Sarawak river which rise 3,000 feet up in the limestone hills and meet fifteen miles lower down. They were constantly changing their ground and he would come upon them in picturesque dells in the mountains, in crevices deep in the rock, or on tower-like summits and craggy pinnacles accessible only by ladders. Sometimes the ore lay in water-worn boulders, 'like eggs in a nest.' More often it lay deep in the clay, from which by extensive trenching and sluicing the persistent Chinese extracted not only antimony but small quantities of gold.

To reach the workings from Kuching took four hours by boat, and Helms waxed lyrical about the journey. The Malays improvised songs as he lay back in the boat, well screened from sun and rain, and admired a scene of tropical nature run riot, untouched by the hand of man. In places the river had worn through the limestone, leaving huge shelving masses overhanging the water, from which trees of fantastic shape sprouted forth to form a cathedral-like vault. A wild tangle of vegetation – orchids, rhododendrons, lilac, tree-ferns as tall as a house – lined the banks and above them all the stately tapang tree towering 150 feet to the first branch. Kingfishers, fireback pheasants, hornbills, doves of yellow, green, and pink, lent colour to the scene and, as night fell, the fireflies 'pulsated like electric sparks flashing from the leaves.'

You cannot, however, inspect antimony workings from a boat, and, when the party stepped ashore, life took on a less utopian pattern. You had to hack your way through creepers and parasites till you chanced on a Dyak path, consisting of rounded slippery bamboos a few inches out of the mud. If you took your eye off the path, and often if you didn't, you slipped waist-deep into mud and were set upon instantly by leeches. Refreshing himself, as he thought, in a cooling stream at the end of a hard day, Helms emerged with twenty-seven. Nor were leeches the only hazard. To snare the game, the Dyaks set traps of a diabolical ingenuity, consisting of a concealed thread across the path and a strong bent-back sapling with a spearhead attached. As you touched the string, the sapling was released and drove the spear horizontally with great force, at an elevation from the ground calculated according to the intended victim. If set for pig, it would pass through a man's leg, but if set for deer, it would, as Helms observed, pass through some more vital part. One could sympathise with his feeling that 'under such circumstances a tropical forest does not inspire the same sentimental enthusiasm as when one views it comfortably reclining in a boat and

The Company's two gold mines in Sarawak. Bidi (below) and the Tai Parit mine at Bau.
When Tai Parit was flooded into extinction in 1923, it had yielded 496,351 ounces of fine gold

perchance reading the latest home news, while the Malays prepare a delicious curry on some pebbly bank in the river . . .'

When he was not exploring, Helms was leading a full life in Kuching, attending the court every Wednesday and giving learned judgments on abstruse cases brought by the litigious Klings – often, as he later learned, not as an end to justice, but as a medium for betting on the result. In the evenings the ailing Rajah would walk his old Arab along the two miles of road which was all that Kuching boasted and would talk over with Helms his dreams for the future of Sarawak.

At this point there occurred two events which, said Helms, 'tended to soothe the Rajah's harassed mind.' One was the appointment of the Reverend F. T. McDougall, head of the Borneo Mission, of whom in heroic aspect we are due to hear more, as Bishop of Sarawak.

The other was the formation of the Borneo Company.

*    *    *

It was a dictum of the first Rajah that in bringing the hand of civilization to the wilder parts of the earth the next most important things after law and order were religion and commerce. He did his best to foster both, and the two were thus brought much into contact with each other, on the one side the Borneo Company and on the other the missionaries, sponsored by the Society for the Propagation of the Gospel. Each was followed by what one may, without disrespect, call 'competitors', but each at first had the field to themselves. As to which had the tougher raw material to work upon – Helms slithering along the 'batang walks' and wading up to his middle in leech-ridden swamps in search of antimony, or the missionaries converting head-hunting Dyaks to an unknown religion in an unknown tongue – it would be difficult to say, but they had one motivating force in common. They believed in what they were doing.

To be a missionary in Borneo a hundred years ago needed faith indeed. When we learn that some of the more ardent propagators of the gospel issued a ration of tobacco to those attending church and provided, as communion wine, 'gin slightly coloured red', and that one Dyak convert, on seeing a picture of the episode of David and Goliath, remarked that the former 'had secured a particularly fine head,' most of us will smile with an indulgence tinged in no way with malice. But it was hard uphill work, and there is no doubt that in this case the end fully justified the means.

The Rajah, who became a little 'difficult' in his later years, had intermittent disputes with the Church, just as he did with the Company, in particular with Bishop McDougall – 'The Mission I believe is much as ever,' he wrote in 1864. 'Peace and charity do not have their abode here' – but he had a robust Christian faith himself and never wavered in his belief that in simple form it could bring much good to his territory. Visiting Chambers, the lone missionary in Banting, who had converted a number of Dyaks, he wondered, 'what will be the effect on them when they find that the uprisings and downsittings, the bendings and genuflections, are not of the importance they attach to them?' He was genuinely pleased that Chambers was making an impression on them which would lead them to Christianity and an advanced civilisation, but, he added, 'they won't be Angels, shut up in a Borneo bandbox, but faulty, erring, sinful, wicked Protestant Christians, like their fellows in England and elsewhere – and they will be much more useful, manly, muscular subjects and citizens in consequence. I hate Monsters of perfection.'

If the Rajah had his ups-and-downs with both, there is no evidence that Church and Company, in their joint hundred years in Sarawak, have ever enjoyed other than the cordial relationship they enjoy today. One of the very first minutes of the Company, in July 1856, relates to the granting of a free passage to a lady about to join the Borneo Female Mission. In that October they voted £200 a year for a new mission school in Sadong and a year or two later a sum of £500 for the Bishop in return for his services to the Company's staff, together with two shares in the Company for his daughters.

The Society for the Propagation of the Gospel, though no longer alone in this field, has provided a century of religious instruction for the people of Sarawak and has received an equally continuous support from the Company, not merely in gifts but in hospitality by members of the one to the other. A witness of this harmonious state of affairs at a time now past the memory perhaps of any other living man is the Venerable Archdeacon Arthur Sharp, who landed at Kuching on Christmas Eve, 1895, and spent the next thirteen years of his life there. Ill health forced him home to England and he became, contrary to all medical advice, vicar of St Stephen's, Hampstead, London, where he remained for ño less than thirty-five years and where he now lives in retirement at the age of nearly ninety. Three years after he went to Hampstead, in 1916, he was offered, and had to decline, the Bishopric of Sarawak. When he was eighty-two, Archdeacon Sharp wrote a charming book of reminiscences, *Wings of the Morning*, and the account of his life in Sarawak, a land which he described as 'one of the noblest enterprises that stand to the credit of the British nation,' contains constant references to the warmth of his welcome by members of the Borneo Company in Kuching and their managers in the remote outstations which he used to visit in order to hold services – evensong in English, matins in Malay.

Visiting him recently, the writer found Archdeacon Sharp a figure venerable indeed and serene, by no means elderly for his years. As he reminisced with remarkable clarity on the semi-civilised Sarawak of sixty years ago, perhaps the outstanding impression that he left was of the complete confidence and safety with which a white man might travel in darkest Borneo in those days. 'The Dyaks and every other tribe,' he said, 'knew that if you were a white man you came as their friend.' It seemed an extraordinary tribute alike to the Rajahs, the Church, and the Borneo Company.

★   ★   ★

Twenty miles up river from Kuching is the now rather pathetic village of Bau. In the early days it was a thriving town, the centre of the Company's mining activities in Sarawak. It was also, indirectly, a cause of their near-extinction almost before they had begun. Chinese had been settled in Bau long before the arrival of Brooke, though they appear to have accepted his suzerainty as Rajah while at the same time retaining a good deal of autonomy in the kongsis, or syndicates, into which they organised themselves. By laborious sluicing operations they extracted enough gold to live on, though only so hard working and thrifty a people could have done it. The amount of country they turned over was prodigious but, as Helms naïvely appraised: 'a Chinaman is willing to work on condition that he is well fed . . . He must have his tea, tobacco, opium, and samsu (a spirit distilled from rice) and, when he has ready money, he must gamble. He is, therefore, an excellent subject to tax, and from the opium, arrack, and gambling farms the Sarawak Treasury was largely replenished. The Dyaks and Malays are but poor subjects to tax; they work little and require little.'

The Chinese are also, however, inveterate smugglers. As anyone familiar

*Borneo types; Land Dyak from Sadong (left) and a Dyak warrior. Within a few years all the Dyaks looked on the white man as their friend*

with the East will testify, smuggling is almost a national pastime. The Sarawak Government retained a monopoly in the opium trade, making on it a respectable profit of 100 per cent – all of which, the moralist may care to observe, was spent in the betterment and development of the country. The community in Bau had been in the habit of taking sixty balls of opium a month. Early in 1857, though the population had increased, the demand for opium through the official channels had fallen unaccountably to thirty balls. Lacking the resources by which to track down the leakage, the authorities ordered that the kongsi should pay, as before, for sixty balls, whether they took them or not.

The result was murder, rape, and destruction; the return of Sarawak for a while to the savagery from which it was beginning so surely to emerge; and the first of the two massive, almost total, disasters to be successfully survived by the Borneo Company.

On the night of 18th February 1857, the little European community – the Rajah and his officers, the Bishop and the missionaries, Helms and the Borneo Company staff, reinforced now by a number of wives from home

– settled peacefully in their beds. What followed is quoted by Helms from the diary of a young friend of his, whose name is left blank and of whom the reader is left to deduce only that he was a member of the Borneo Company and a bachelor. Nothing could reveal more graphically the hazards of life in Borneo a hundred years ago.*

At half-past one in the morning of 19th February, Tidman was woken by a young lady with a weak voice saying: 'The Bishop says, if you please will you get up and bring your gun.' He rushed downstairs to find a general state of alarm, the sound of gunfire in the bazaar, the Bishop and men-servants busy loading.

'The Chinese are down from Bau,' said the Bishop, 'and are attacking the town'.

In the house were six men and eight women. 'That all could escape, no one had the least idea. The only thing to be done was to make the best defence possible. Besides, the prospect of dying fighting was less unsatis-factory than that of being murdered in cold blood.' The Bishop said a short prayer and gave them a blessing for, as all thought, the last time. Mean-while, the Rajah's house and the bungalow-annexe were blazing. So were two others, including that of Crookshank, the magistrate, against whom the

---

* The diarist was in fact Paul Tidman, who had come out to the East only in the previous year and was no  twenty. Tidman stayed eight years in the East and on returning to London founded the firm of Mactaggart and Tidman, East India merchants. He was also practically the founder of the Bi-Metallic League. He died at Chislehurst, Kent, in 1889.

*Turning point in Sarawak history: the Company retakes Kuching (Water-colour by Helms)*

Chinese bore a special animosity. Rumour had it that the Rajah was dead, but in fact he and his party had escaped through a back way, swum the creek, and retired down the river. One of his staff, Nicholetts, confronting the raiders as he came out of the annexe, was instantly killed. Crookshank tried to shield his wife but a man ran a spear through her from behind and she fell as though dead, while Crookshank, himself wounded, escaped into the jungle. She was later brought in alive, robbed of her rings. Helms escaped through his back door and, returning next day, was informed by a local Chinese that Mrs Middleton was in the jungle, so he went out and brought her in. Her husband, who as chief of police came into frequent contact with the smugglers, had thought it at first an attack only personally on himself and had bolted into the jungle. When the Chinese made their way into the house, a young metallurgist of the Borneo Company, Wellington, opposed them and, though he killed one man with the butt end of his gun, he himself was in turn quickly killed. On the roll of honour of thirty-five men who have lost their lives in the service of the Company, the first name is that of Wellington.

By morning the Chinese were in possession of the town and a conference of capitulation was held in the court-house, the kongsi's leader sitting on his haunches in the Rajah's chair. The kongsi declared they had no wish to interfere with the Europeans, claimed immunity from taxes, and elected Helms Rajah – an honour which he respectfully declined. Eventually they agreed that the Chinese should withdraw up the river with their plunder, the Malays should not attack them on the way, and no boats should be sent after them. The contract was written out in three languages and sealed, Chinese fashion, by cutting off the heads of two fowls and, as they fluttered about the table, sprinkling their blood on the documents.

'After which,' says Tidman, 'came tea and cigars, and we had to sit another half hour drinking and smoking, and, when we left, were obliged to shake hands with the brutes whom with the greatest of pleasure we could have shot dead on the spot.'

After sundry skirmishes the Chinese left next day but general disorder ensued, the infuriated Malays, 'not being in the humour to distinguish one Chinese tail from another,' chivvying the guiltless Chinese traders in the bazaar. A note came up from the Rajah saying, 'The schooner *Good Luck* is down the river. Hasten on board and write to Harvey (the Borneo Company manager in Singapore) to send us arms and ammunition. I will be with you tomorrow with plenty of men. Meanwhile hold the fort' – an instruction which, as the diarist remarks, was like telling the Israelites to make bricks without straw. 'But for the Bishop,' he goes on, 'there would have been chaos. He was commander-in-chief and organised everything . . . like us all, he was armed to the teeth, with sword, double-barrel, and revolver. He recalled the olden times when lord-bishops could strike a blow, if need be, in a good cause.'

News came that the kongsi were coming down the river again and nothing could stop a general stampede. The Rajah came up the river in a solitary boat with no men at all, was fired at by the kongsi, and retired up the coast leaving a message for Helms, 'Offer the country, on any terms, to the Dutch.' The fifth morning after the original attack saw the survivors assembled in a variety of craft at the mouth of the river, gazing sadly at the distant smoke rising from Sarawak and preparing to make for the island of Serasan, two days from the mainland and governed by a native sultan with whose aid they hoped to reach Singapore. At this moment, as the men were hoisting sail, came a turning point in the history of Sarawak.

Cries of 'Kapalapi! Kapalapi!' (the steamer! the steamer!) brought every man on deck and 'never was a more welcome sight vouchsafed to anyone. The effect on us was quite beyond my power to describe. The Malays danced for joy and my hat went spinning in the air . . .' They thought it was a Dutchman and that they would have to 'offer the country', but it was not. It was Captain Skinner and the Borneo Company's steamer, called appropriately enough the *Sir James Brooke*.

Helms, deemed 'acting Rajah' whether he liked it or not, decided to advance on the town at once. Rifles and cutlasses were being issued and the decks cleared when the Rajah himself returned, having seen the steamer's smoke. On approaching the fort they were greeted with a blast of grape shot consisting of balls, nails, and rusty iron, but a moment later the 18-pounder, manned by the mate, replied with a mighty roar and in a matter of minutes the fort was cleared.

'Out scoured the Chinese like wild hares in March, some dashing up the road, others running through the bazaar, affording practice for the riflemen on board. We steamed slowly up the river, on the side of which the Malay kampong was still burning, and then coming back again anchored off the bazaar. And thus the Company's steamer retook the town of Sarawak.'

Confusion reigned supreme, though all were delighted to see Russell, the

*Robert Henderson, of Glasgow, first Chairman of the Borneo Company, 1856 (left), and John Harvey, the Company's first managing director in the East*

Company's manager at the Bidi mines, long since given up for lost, safe after a fortnight in Dyak villages. An armed search of the town produced twelve captives, one of whom was summarily convicted in the court-house and already had five or six spears sticking in him by the time his head was cut off on the green outside. The Sea Dyaks were in with their warboats, pulled at great speed by thirty men at a time, and were with difficulty deterred from setting off after the kongsi forthwith in search of heads. Instead they crowded on the steamer, examining everything and expressing great astonishment, while an eccentric spinster on board 'afforded unceasing amusement by her unequivocal admiration of these lightly-clad warriors.'

As the days passed, nothing could restrain either the Malays or the Sea Dyaks. The Malay chief took a party up the river and massacred a stockade-full of Chinese and a few nights later the Dyaks returned chanting in a fashion which indicated all too clearly the nature of their prize. Tidman in his diary described the scene on the morrow as the most disgusting part of the whole affair.

'The heads, after being cleaned, are hung over a slow fire and smoked; this effectually cures them and they are then ready for stacking. Perhaps thirty heads were hanging in different parts of the bazaar today. The Dyaks seem to take a particular pleasure in superintending the cooking in front of the Chinese in the bazaar and when any of these came up to recognise an acquaintance, maybe a friend, they looked as much as to say, "If it were not for the very great respect we entertain for the fire-ship's guns, we should feel the greatest pleasure in adding your head to this little collection." '

A few days later the Borneo Company's sailing vessel *Water Lily* arrived with the message: 'By this schooner we ship arms, ammunition, and stores for the Sarawak Government, also specie for account of the Borneo Company. Out of this remittance you will please furnish the Rajah with such sum of money as he may require; and generally you are authorised to place at the disposal of the Sarawak Government the whole resources of the Company in Borneo, so far as they may be made available for the upholding of the Government and the safety of the European and other residents in the Rajah's territory.'

So ended, after little more than a twelvemonth, the first phase of the Company's hundred years in Borneo. We may pay tribute in retrospect to the gallant little band of pioneers, and in particular to the memory of young Wellington, but the beginning was inauspicious indeed.

★    ★    ★

Meanwhile Singapore remained the commercial core of the Company and the administrative heart of the enterprise, as a glance at the first profit and loss accounts of 1857, set out on pages 14–15, abundantly show. They were prepared to go in for anything that came their way, large or small – as indeed they are today. One moment they were advertising 'Milner's Fire Proof Safes, of all sizes' or '290 tons of TEAK, assorted Squares, Planks or Boards'. At another, also in 1857, a notice in the *Straits Times* signed 'Zavala, Consul for Spain,' announced 'THE BORNEO COMPANY LIMITED have been instructed to sell 1,052 tons, 10 cwts 2 qrs and 17 lb of COAL, belonging to Her Catholic Majesty's Government, and those who may be desirous of purchasing the same will have to settle with this Company.'

No greater compliment to the roving spirit and ubiquitous quest for business of Harvey and his early associates could have been paid than the disagreeable editorial which appeared in the *Hong Kong Daily News* of 10th June 1858, and was duly reprinted in the *Straits Times:*

'The Borneo Company Limited does not limit its operations to Borneo and would appear to have about as legitimate a claim to the title as those Catholic prelates have, who, being appointed by the Pope to the spiritual supervision of heathen countries often unexplored and dangerous to visit, are dignified by the title of Bishop or Vicar Apostolic of the district marked on the map as their see. If a comparison is to be made between the arbitrary and often assumed titles of the Vatican, and the applicability of that adopted by the above-named Company, it certainly cannot be denied that the Church has the preponderance of reason and common-sense on its side. If, for instance, the Pope were to appoint a bishop to Borneo, conferring on him of course the title of his see, the right reverend father would enter upon his functions if he possibly could. If he could not, he would hardly become excursive in his prelacy and take under his episcopal charge Siam, Singapore, Calcutta, China, or whatever other places might suit his fancy.'

That such a Company should own ships and steamers, the editor of the *Hong Kong Daily News* thought fair enough. That it should employ them in any other trade as carriers when the Borneo trade should happen to be dull was also quite legitimate and proper. He would even go to the length of placing the whole Eastern Archipelago at the mercy of the Directors of the Company to experimentalise upon, but further than that, he said, he would object to go.

'A Company trading under the names of individuals has, of course, a perfect right to do what it likes with its own . . . and it would be impertinent in any journal to question its exercising it. But for a company trading under a corporate appellation to embark on operations quite contrary to its cognomen constitutes a subject on which the public have a right to be correctly informed. It appears that this Borneo Company not only trades in the capacity of an untrammelled individual with as much regard to Borneo as to any other places in which he might have business relations, but it is also embarking large sums in the erection of machinery in Bengal for the purpose of saving the flax, which the native method of extracting the

*The first Singapore office, a hundred years ago – very different from the imposing building standing there today*

33

*Left, Samuel Gilfillan, first manager in Bangkok; and, right, the man who introduced Anna to the King of Siam – William Adamson, Borneo Company manager in Singapore, 1862*

seed destroys. Such an enterprise is, of course, highly laudable, but what in the name of all that is consistent has the Borneo Company to do with it?'

Without wishing to do injustice to the anonymous writer, one cannot look back on the picture of Hong Kong only a few years after the opium war without suspecting that he was not there solely for the good of his health or to edit a daily news sheet. More likely he had been beaten on the post in a commercial venture of his own by an enterprising member of the Borneo Company.

Be that as it may, the Company were certainly in Calcutta, Batavia, and Siam in the earliest days and for a time they also had branches in Hong Kong and Shanghai. The latter seems to have made little impact on the Company's fortunes but for a while Hong Kong played a considerable and useful part. The branch opened in 1856 and its main business was exporting baled silk and importing rice from Siam. Later, as the Tegora mercury mines were opened up in Sarawak, the Hong Kong branch became the main centre for distributing cinnabar and quicksilver in the Far East. Cinnabar is a rich red ore and found great popularity as a cosmetic with the ladies of China, who presumably learnt from bitter experience the devastating effects of the continuous use of mercury on the human system. At any rate, as the mercury mine gradually declined, business in Hong Kong seems to have dwindled too and the branch was closed in 1890.

Calcutta, however, became quite a big affair. The Company's Barnagore jute factory was the first of its kind in India, and in 1857 they also bought a sugar refinery at Bally-Khan which was later converted to paper milling. They ran them themselves for more than half a century, then floated them as separate companies, and finally in the twenties released direct interest in them. When they ceased their connection for the Barnagore jute in 1935 it was the end of eighty years continuous association with the jute interests in Dundee.*

The Company were also in Batavia in the 1850s – there was talk in 1862 of shipping mules from Montevideo for the Batavia branch but this, perhaps just as well, was not proceeded with – and they have been in the Dutch East Indies, now entitled Indonesia, with varying ups and downs for the whole of their hundred years.

Still, Singapore was the centre of the web. The population in 1860, as estimated by the police, was 80,000, of which only 2,500 odd were European or Eurasian, and 50,000 Chinese. The new harbour, comprising the wharves at Telok Blanga and 148 acres of land which Harvey seems to have brought with him almost as his personal property on joining the Company, was to become the biggest thing of its kind in the Far East. This property divided the two existing dock companies of the time. It was floated as a separate company in 1863, with Samuel Gilfillan representing the BCL on the board, and three years later the capital had to be doubled – 'no one then anticipating what the Company would grow into in the next thirty years.' In July 1885 the Borneo Company sold out to the Tanjong Pagar Dock Company – one of its original two neighbours – for a million dollars. The deal was subject to conditions on either side – the new owners undertaking to provide berths for the war steamers and transports of the French navy, for whom the BCL were agents, and the Company in turn undertaking not

*The memory, however, lingers on in that part of the world. When the writer recently let fall the words 'Borneo Company' in the Royal and Ancient clubhouse at St Andrews, ears pricked up on every side.

to interest themselves in any rival wharves for twenty-five years. In 1905 the Tanjong Pagar Dock Company was taken over by the Government and is today represented by the Singapore Harbour Board. Until comparatively recently part of the Board's property was still known as Borneo Wharf. One hardly likes to contemplate what Harvey's original property would be worth today.

On the lighter side of Singapore life it was noted that 'of light comedians none excelled William Adamson, in melodrama Mr de la Feuillade of the Borneo Company excelled . . . and as a delineator of female characters Mr William Mulholland of the Borneo Company was never surpassed.' However, life was not all fun and games. One firm failed for a million dollars and the Chartered Bank only survived the consequent run on its funds by paying all cheques in silver, often in sackfuls, instead of notes.

However, if Singapore were the centre of the web and of social life, the hard slogging was still being done in Borneo, and now at last it was beginning to show practical results. Complaining of the damage done to the Sarawak trade by reports of piracy which investigation showed to be groundless, the *Straits Times* in May 1869 said: 'considering that the trade from Sarawak in the past year amounted to two millions of dollars, the greater part of which was shipped to Singapore, it must be to the interest of the British Government to foster a trade increasing year by year . . . Sarawak being essentially a producing country, each year shows some new and valuable discovery of products suitable to the home and eastern markets and the opening of the cinnabar mines discovered by Mr Helms, the Borneo Company's manager, which are undoubtedly the richest discovered in modern times, has given a great impetus to the labour market. Over five hundred Chinese, to say nothing of Malays, Dyaks, and other races, are engaged in working the ore, of which two valuable shipments have already been made, and more than two thousand Chinese immigrants have arrived during the past year.'

\* \* \*

At this point we may pause to follow the Company a hundred years ago to a land of unlimited promise and enchantment, namely Siam. Here it had not been a question of combating a land of savages and jungle, as in Borneo, but of getting on terms with a people who combined many centuries of

*His Majesty King Chulalongkorn of Siam, 1853–1910. The first monarch of Siam to travel outside his country, he visited Europe in 1897*

*A letter written by King Mongkut to Samuel Gilfillan, the Company's manager in Siam,*

culture with a deep mistrust of European influence. Several attempts had been made, among others by James Brooke, to come to terms with the Siamese, but the answer had in every case been implacably in the negative. Rumour reached Singapore in 1851 that the reigning King had died and been succeeded by one who took a more enlightened view of opening up the country to western commerce, and in that year some Singapore merchants sent up none other than our old friend Helms – it was long before he came into the Borneo picture – to find out if it were true.

Briefly, it was. Helms was received in tremendous state by the new King, Somdet Phra Parra-Manda* – a man 'past middle age, thin, fair complexioned and with an air of good nature' – and ended with a letter of compliments and thanks; an invitation to settle in Siam; an order, so he said, for twenty thousand pounds' worth of arms; and a golden flower, presented by the second, or deputy, King; which is now in the possession of Helms' granddaughter in Dorset.

*Helms'· spelling. The King's correct title was Somdetch Phra Paramendr Maha Mongkut. He was known and referred to as King Mongkut.

as he was an orphan who has lost his father at his country & on consequence of the quarelsomeness with his kindred has got down here & took refuge & lives under me two years ago & unfortunately died here himself on November ult; but on consequence of waiting for arrival of his sons who were remained in his country, his remains

were kept in gilt coffine a corps box at his residence here until th— arrival of his Sons who were just arrived here four days ago. I beg therefore to remove the appointment again to be on next Tuesday 4 P.M.

I beg to remain your faithful & wel wisher S.P.P.M. Mongkut R S R y 3545 days ago

*in 1858. His Majesty desires to postpone an interview through having to attend a funeral*

A trickle of trade began between Singapore and Bangkok and in 1856 – a red letter day in the history not merely of the Borneo Company but also of Siam – Sir John Bowring, Her Majesty's Plenipotentiary in China, signed a treaty with King Mongkut. The latter stands as one of the great figures in Siamese history. He saw with remarkable clarity that, far from being incompatible, national sovereignty and western commerce could combine to bring to Siam a prosperity undreamed of by his people. The Borneo Company, in the person of Gilfillan, who as usual had started as 'one of the clerks', was first in the field and thus began a century-old partnership which for continuous success and goodwill can have few equals in the annals of commerce.

The earliest recorded correspondence between the royal house of Siam and the Company, dated 2nd September, 1856, is addressed by King Mongkut, in his own hand in English, to MacEwen and Company; though they had by that time lost their identity in the Borneo Company. It proves that their tentacles had stretched out as far as Bangkok even before the signing of the treaty. It is also proof of the King's new policy.

*The real Anna, Mrs Anna Harriette Leonowens, at the time of her engagement by King Mongkut through The Borneo Company*

No. 149 of our royal Manuscrit
in the year 1856 which is
the six of our reign.

———

Somdetch Phra Paramendr Maha Mongkut by the blessing of Superagency of
the universe the king of Siam & Sovereign of Laos Etc. Etc.
To MacEwen & Co. at firm of Messrs. late Hamilton Grey perhaps of Singapore.
Senth greetings!
Sirs your letter under the date of 21st August inst accompanied a parcel
contains 4 articles mentioned in latter part of the letter sent me by Mr. Martin on
the 1st September inst. was received.
I beg to return my many sincere thanks to you and Mr. Martin for being in so
good kindness toward me as to let me have useful articles for our good copying
and employment of phylosophical instruments.
I beg to assure you that I will do my favourable attention to Mr. Gilfillan we
will transact your matters of benefit here by suitable assistance.
He wrote me to grant the exportation of the 2,000 Koyains of rice. I have then
immediately sent him our proclamation issued for opening of the export of rice
from hence to abroad.
I beg to enclose herewith two copies of our proclamation for the exporting of
rice among our people, trusting they will be in your inspection of leaning of its
content from translation of any Siamese interpriter of your port.
Also I will supply to the exporting of Mr Gilfillan herewith certain number of
Koyains of white rice of first quality in assistance to your firm's purpose and trust
you will perceive our being gratitude.
Given in our court of Amarindr Winichai grand palace Bangkok on the 2nd
day of September 1856, which is the six of our reign.

Not that all was plain sailing in the early days. The voyage from Singapore to Bangkok was liable to take several weeks and Europeans had to live
aboard their own vessels, moored perhaps in mid-river beside the vast fleet
of Chinese junks which formed a kind of bazaar on their own and for two
months each year were one of the sights of Bangkok. What is now the
modern city, whose history is synonymous with that of the Borneo Company, was a tract of scrub. Apart from a few lanes in the old walled city,
communication everywhere was by boat along the klongs – the innumerable
waterways by which, the water being everywhere but a few feet below
ground level, Bangkok is intersected and on which and in which so many of
its citizens live a homely, unsophisticated, but in many ways idyllic,
existence to this day. There were no harbour regulations, no pilot service

มีพระบรมราชโองการ ให้ประ
กาษแก่ข้าราชการแลราษฎร ใน
กรุงนอกกรุงทั้งปวงให้รู้ทั่วกัน
ด้วยเมื่อค้นบี้นี้ ทรงพระราชกำ
ริห์พร้อมกับความคิดท่านเสนา
บดี่เหนว่า ฝนค้นบี้มี่มากผิด
ปรกคิกลัวฝนกลางมื้อจะแล้งรา
คาเข้าจะขึ้นไป จึ่งให้บีดเข้า
มิให้ซายออกนอกประเทศ ตั้ง
แต่เคือนห้าขึ้นค่ำหนึ่งมา ก็ถึง
๔ เคือนแล้ว บัดนี้ก็เปนเวลา
ฝนกลางมื้อแล้ว ฝนก็ยังตกประ
ปรายเสมออยู่เข้าในนาก็งามดีทุก
คำบล ราคาเข้าก็หาขึ้นแรงไป
ไม่ครั้นจะบีดต่อไปอีกก็กลัวราษ
ฎรเหนว่าเข้าถูกนัก จะทิ้ง

ไร่นาไปไม่ทำการอื่นเสียทรงพระเมคาปรานีแก่ราษฎร จึ่งโปรดเก้ลาโปรดกระหม่อม ให้ประกาษไปครั้งหนึ่ง
ให้เตรียมขึ้นเข้าไว้ให้ภอใช้สอย อย่าต้องบ่นว่าเพราะเบ็ดเข้าอยกนอกประเทศราคาเข้าจึ้งขึ้นไป ได้ความ
ยากแก่ผู้ที่มิได้ทำนา ประกาษก็นานถึงเคือนหนึ่งแล้วราคาเข้าก็ยังคงอยู่ ให้ราษฎรซายเข้าแก่
นา ๆ ประเทศได้ตามใจ คนนอกประเทศที่เปนไมคริ์กับกรุงก็จะได้ผลประโยชน์ตามประสงค์บ้าง
ควัยทรงพระเมคากรุณาแก่คนในพระราชอานาเขตร แลจวก่างประเทศที่เย่นมิตรไมคริ์นั้นคล้ายกัน
จึ่งโปรดเก้ลาโปรดกระหม่อมให้ประกาษบัดนี้ว่า ตั้งแต่เคือนเก้าไปไม่ห้ามไม่บีดแก่คนนอกประเทศแล้ว
เมื่อฝนปลายมื้อแล้งไปนักราษฎรทำมาได้นัย เข้าในกรุงมีราคาแพงมากขึ้นนักจึ่งจะให้บีดเข้าเสียมิให้ซาย
ก้ัดคนนอกประเทศอีกเมื่อใดจะห้ามจึ่งจะพิมพ์ประกาษห้ามต่อภายหลัง ประกาษ
มาณวันเสาระเคือนเก้าขึ้นค่ำหนึ่ง ปี้มโรงนักษัตรอรุ้ศก ๆะ

## KING MONGKUT'S PROCLAMATION
## LIFTING EXPORT BAN ON RICE

---

By Command of His Majesty it is hereby proclaimed to officials and citizens in and outside the City that:

Whereas at the beginning of the present year, with the advice of the Ministers, His Majesty deemed that as the rains at the beginning of the monsoon were abnormally heavy they might later become abnormally light, and therefore the export sale of rice to outside the Kingdom had to be prohibited from the first day of the waning moon of the fifth month, which is now four months past.

Whereas, now in the middle of the monsoon, the rains have been fairly steady and rice is plentiful in all districts, and furthermore rice prices have not risen.

Therefore should the prohibition be continued it might cause citizens, believing that rice prices would fall greatly, to abandon their fields to take up other occupation against the bountiful wish of His Majesty.

Furthermore, by His Majesty's Command it has been proclaimed once before that:

All should prepare to buy sufficient rice for their own use.

No complaints should be made that rice prices would increase, creating difficulties for those not engaged in rice growing, when export sale of rice to outside the Kingdom were to be permitted.

This proclamation was made over one month ago and rice prices are still steady.

Therefore citizens should be permitted to sell rice to various nations as they may wish.

People outside the Kingdom friendly with this City will then reap the benefits of His Majesty's grace and bounty towards the people of the Kingdom, and foreigners who are friendly will also reap similar benefits.

Therefore be it proclaimed by His Majesty's Command that:

As from the ninth month it is not forbidden nor prohibited for people outside the Kingdom to buy rice.

Should the rains at the end of the monsoon season become low and citizens produce less rice, and rice in the City become expensive, the prohibition may be re-enforced, forbidding the sale of rice to people outside the Kingdom.

Such prohibition will be proclaimed later, when necessary, by printed proclamation.

Proclaimed on Saturday the first day of the rising moon of the ninth month in the year of the Big Snake (July 1856).

and, perhaps the greatest deterrent of all, no insurance facilities beyond the bar of the Menam, forty miles below Bangkok.

Nevertheless, the trickle of trade turned almost into a torrent as one firm after another, American, British, German, and French (the French had an embassy in Siam in the days of 'Siamese White' in the mid-1600s) swarmed in to follow the Borneo Company. A few early fortunes were made, but twenty-five years later there were no American firms left in Siam, practically no other British, and only one or two French and German.

When Gilfillan arrived, he was already the accredited agent of Lloyds, and it is probably fair to attribute the foundations of the Company's prosperity in Siam to insurance. At any rate, in the next year or two they had three other important agencies, and to this day it remains notable among

*Anna's son, T. L. Leonowens (left), who spent some years developing teak concessions for the Company in Northern Siam. Later he founded the firm which bears his name today*

*His Majesty King Mongkut of Siam (left) and King Mongkut's Foreign Minister, or 'Kromatah'*

their activities in the Far East. They soon went into the steam rice milling business, although forestalled by an American firm whose mill, the first in Siam, was a financial failure, and the Company's steam mill, twice burnt down and twice enlarged, was a feature of the commercial life of Bangkok till, like other Europeans, they sold out to the Chinese.

Progress went steadily along. In 1868 they were representing three banking houses – one of them the National Bank of Scotland. They went in for saw-milling and steam towing and ran a coastal service every fourth Tuesday down the coast from Bangkok. For a long time they had the purchase and marketing of pepper from Chantaboon to themselves, and when sapphires brought further prominence to the place they carried nearly 5,000 passengers in six months. In twenty years the whole life, outlook, and appearance of Bangkok had changed and, as the Royal House of Siam has graciously acknowledged over the years, the Borneo Company were mainly responsible for changing it.

For the Bangkok of 1874 we have, by extraordinary luck, an eye-witness whose story is in every way as vivid as that of Helms. He is Robert Henderson, of Randalls Park, Leatherhead, Surrey, son of the original chairman and the third of no fewer than nine Hendersons who have been directors of the Company. One of his sons was the Sir Nevile Henderson who was ambassador in Berlin at the outbreak of the second world war. Today there is not only a Henderson on the board but also Ian MacEwen, a descendant of the original MacEwens of a hundred years ago.

Henderson set off round the world in January 1874, and his journal, beautifully bound and running to nearly 500 typewritten pages, is before me now. It radiates the enthusiasm of an age when 'foreign parts' were new and, though a mere fraction of it refers to the present story in Siam or Borneo, I find I have read it from cover to cover.

Henderson reached the bar of the Menam in September in the 800-ton stern-wheeler *Kromatah* carrying 'betel nut, iron nails, piece goods and other odds and ends.' A lighthouse had now been built at the bar and was to be opened on the 10th, the Prince of Wales' birthday. They were towed up by the Company's steamer *Sanspareil*, Captain Lesson, who remarked that their steamer *Weazle* had been thrown away at 7,000 dollars in Singapore and would have fetched 10,000 in Bangkok and furthermore that the Company's coal was almost unburnable. Henderson noted vast tracts of

*The first Bangkok office, a hundred years ago*

*Left, Anna Leonowens, dignified and handsome in her sixties; and, right, the seated Buddha at Ayuthia, Siam (member of Company in foreground)*

well cultivated paddy fields and the best native residences he had yet seen. Landing at the Borneo Company wharf, he strolled around, noting the office close to the house, with the wharf in front, three long godowns behind, and the Company's cows grazing in a meadow. The manager, F. S. Clarke, was absent playing the organ to a congregation of twelve in church. Later they inspected the rice mill and other property and the grave of the late manager, Mr John Blyth, the only manager to die in service in Bangkok in a hundred years. Although there were so few Europeans there, Henderson noted, they had nearly all quarrelled and were hardly on speaking terms, 'the BCL being apparently the only neutral house.'

He got on well with the Siamese, a number of whom had been to Oxford, though he found them liable to be 'very keen on a thing for a short time and then give it up and let it go to rack and ruin.' He had some good nostalgic talk with the chief engineer, Howarth, who was an excellent oar, had been in the champion four of Scotland and 'knew Phelps,' and met Captain Orton, brother of the famous Tichborne claimant, who commanded the *Chao Phya*, one of the Company's up-river towing steamers.

He was also, of course, greeted with plenty of criticism. Fancy the

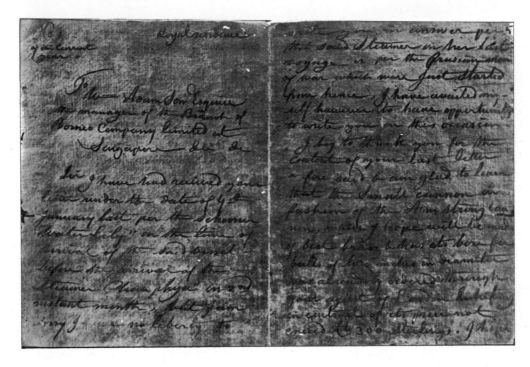

*King Mongkut's letter, in his own hand to William Adamson, manager of the Company*

Singapore branch buying Barnagore gunny bags in the open market when every branch could so easily get a regular supply direct from Calcutta and then, in Bangkok at any rate, get the monopoly of the market! If only they were allowed a little more latitude, there was no limit to the opportunities they could seize. Instead they had to wire repeatedly to London and 'the home people take no further notice than to acknowledge the telegram.'*

At any rate, criticism or no, the Company, now twenty years old, was firmly on its feet, Bangkok was well on its way to becoming the great city it is today, and we may pause in the narrative to note a truly enchanting little episode. Perhaps little is hardly the word, for in the era of mass entertainment which was to come exactly ninety years later the episode was to capture

*A complaint common, in the writer's experience, to all great trading concerns, to say nothing of Her Majesty's Forces, where instructions from the General Staff are widely held by the man in the field to be pointless, sometimes insane – till the recipient is himself appointed to the Staff. In March, 1865, the London directors of the Borneo Company issued instructions to all branch managers that the Directors' orders 'shall not only be implicitly obeyed, but without any cavilling on your part'!

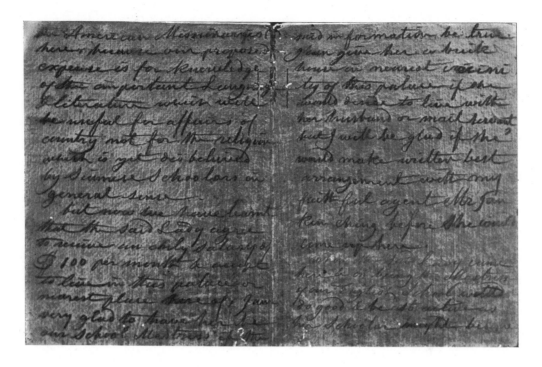

the imagination of many millions of people in all parts of the world.

In 1862 the Borneo Company introduced Anna to the King of Siam.

★     ★     ★

By an extraordinary coincidence the two women who became the most celebrated royal governesses in history bore the same name – Anna Harriette Crawford, born in Caernarvon in 1834, and Marion Crawford, the 'Crawfie' of the nursery days of Princesses Elizabeth and Margaret.

Anna's father was killed on active service in India when she was six, and at the age of fifteen she went out there to join her mother. She fell in love at once with the dashing, if penurious, Major Thomas Louis Leonowens, and married him in Bombay in 1851. Their first child, Avis, was born when Anna was seventeen and the second, Louis – who was to feature, somewhat unsatisfactorily alas, in the Borneo Company's story – a year later.

The love letters between the two when service life in India kept them apart are, to the writer at least, the most enchanting part in Miss Margaret Landon's book *Anna and the King of Siam*, which was to bring Mrs Leonowens world-wide fame on stage and screen so many years after her death.

Their romance was tragically short-lived. Leonowens was ordered to Singapore and there they learned daily of the death of their friends and of Anna's relatives in the Indian Mutiny. Banks failed all over India and with them vanished Anna's small private fortune. Then, the crowning blow, Leonowens himself collapsed and died after a tiger hunt in Johore. His brother officers raffled his belongings and gave her the proceeds, but soon she and the two children, then six and five, were penniless. The girl was sent home to England, while Anna opened a school for officers' children and tried listlessly to resume normal life. It was soon after this, in 1862, that King Mongkut asked his agent in Singapore to find an English governess for the royal children. William Adamson, manager of the Borneo Company, later Sir William and the one who had 'not been excelled as a light comedian' in Singapore, suggested Anna.

Palace life in Bangkok, as readers of Miss Landon's book will vividly recall, was a mixture of beauty and barbarity. King Mongkut had one foot, as it were, in the despotic past, and the other in an almost scholarly future. He turned lightly from the whipping of slave girls to grappling with the English language, for much of which he relied direct upon the dictionary. It is true that he went into a tantrum for a week on seeing himself described in the *Bangkok Times* as a 'spare' man, taking it to mean 'superfluous', but considering the sparseness of English-speaking residents, his letters, many of which are preserved by the Borneo Company, are a delightful combination of quaintness and skill. The handwriting is beautiful and to have these letters in one's possession, to pore over them while imagining the scene as the King burned the midnight oil composing them in his palace and penning them on these very sheets of paper, has been, to the writer, one of the most intriguing experiences in tracing the Borneo Company story.

In 1862 the King wrote a long letter to Adamson. He enquires first about a small two-inch cannon that the Company had ordered for him in London, price not to exceed £300 sterling, and goes on about a breech loading brass cannon and 1,000 rounds of ball ammunition that he understands Sir James Brooke to have put up for sale on his return to England. He has also, he says, run out of the excellent cough lozenges (correctly spelt), which the Company have been sending him and requests another half dozen bottles – 'I wish but those which are genuine' – to be sent up by the *Chao Phya*. The next paragraphs concern Anna and, since the day that Adamson introduced her to the King's attention was to have so profound an influence directly on the future of Siam, they shall be quoted in full. Parts of the original letter may be seen in facsimile on pages 48–49.

'My faithful agent Mr Tan Kim Ching has told me in his letter to me that you and your lady has introduced Mrs Leonowens to him with an application that she will be English School Mastriss here under the salary of $150 per month and her residence shall be near of Protestant Missionary here. For this we are hesitating on the subject considering that our English School will be just established and may be very small so the required salary seemed to be higher than what we proposed although proper because everything here cheaper than there at Singapore, also we wish the School Mastriss to be with us in this palace or nearest vicinity hereof to save us from trouble of conveying such the Lady to & fro, almost every day also it is not pleasant to us if the School Mastriss much more endeavour to convert the scholars to Christianity than teaching Language literature &c. &c. like American Missionaries here because our proposed expense is for knowledge of the important Language & literature which will be useful for affairs of country not for the religion which is yet disbelieved by Siamese Schoolars in general sense.

but now we have learnt that the said Lady agree to receive an only salary of $100 per month & accept to live in this palace or nearest place hereof, I am very glad to have her be our School Mastriss if the said information be true. I can give her a brick house in nearest vicinity of this palace if she would decide to live with her husband or maid-servant, but I will be glad if she would make written best arrangement with my faithful agent Mr Tan Kim Ching before she would come up here.

When the said Lady came here & on being the Mastriss of our English School would do good & be so active as her Schoolar might become in facility of language literature quickly & the study of School might so increase as I would see her labour heavier than what we expected, myself will reward her some time or add her salary in suitable portion.'

The King concluded his letter, 'Trusting you will see that my attention is in assistance to your firm always and will thank me for the same and beg to remain your good friend and well wisher, &c.'

The story of Anna is tolerably familiar. She must indeed have been a remarkable woman. An attractive girl in her twenties, she lived alone in Bangkok with her young son – standing up to the King's rages and to court intrigue in an atmosphere where to others a false move meant instant removal to the dungeon, or worse; teaching the royal children; comforting the slaves; acting as secretary; constantly called out in the middle of the night to dress and hurry over to the Palace, only to find that the King was stuck for a single English word. Her real impact on Siam, however, came when in 1868 the King died and was succeeded by the young Prince Chulalongkorn, whom she had taught all through his formative years. The gradual abolition of slavery is traceable directly to the influence of Anna on the young Prince and to her teaching that true greatness lay in those who endured suffering, not those who with a wave of the hand could inflict it on others. Though no one could have guessed it at the time, the day that Adamson of the Borneo Company said to Tan Kim Ching, 'What about Mrs Leonowens?' was a turning point in the history of Siam.

Though she had an affectionate meeting with her old pupil when King Chulalongkorn was in London in 1897, having then reigned twenty-nine years, Anna herself left Siam in 1867 to recuperate from the rigours of her five years in Bangkok and was in Ireland when the old King died. She and her two children went with friends to New York, thinking to return to Siam that way, but in fact she never went back. An article in the *Atlantic Monthly* in 1869 and two books of reminiscences put her in great demand as a lecturer, just as they would today, and she even went to Russia for *The Youth's Companion* to write a series of articles after the assassination of Alexander II. Avis set up a kindergarten in New York, while Louis, a rolling stone if ever there was one, decided that America 'was played out' and departed for Australia, where he entered the police force – a tough assignment, as one would imagine, in the seventies. At any rate, he was soon on his travels again, and in 1882 completed his encirclement of the globe by turning up again in Siam. King Chulalongkorn made him an officer in the cavalry, sending a message to Anna through the Siamese Consul in New York that he was happy to do so for her sake, and very soon afterwards Louis re-entered the story of the Borneo Company.

★     ★     ★

This romantic interlude over, let us retrace our steps and return to Borneo, where the Rajah, the Company, and the missionaries have almost, as it were, been knocked out in the first round.

*On the way from the quicksilver mines at Tegora; the tunnel at Jambusan*

Peace, of a sort, had been restored after the Chinese rising, but for a year or two life in Sarawak was to be anti-climax. How pleasant it had been, Helms recorded, 'to see steamers on our jungle-surrounded rivers, and energetic Englishmen, fresh from home, full of eagerness for work, to enliven our small circle . . . to myself new prospects had suddenly been opened; the tender plant which I had been nursing for so many years was under a forcing system and great resources had been placed at my disposal'. He had been ten years in the East and had suffered in health. Furthermore, his arrangements with the new Company required adjustment, which could only be done in London, and in June 1858 he set sail for Europe.

Within the year he had engaged to return as Borneo Company manager in Sarawak and left Southampton on 20th February, 1860. So rapid had been the improvements in sea travel in the fifties that he now reached Sarawak in fifty-six days. On his first voyage he had taken 163 days merely to reach Singapore.

He found things in a 'low and desponding condition.' Many Europeans had left or were packing to go. The neighbouring chieftain in Muka, where Helms had his eye on developing sago, had banned Sarawak traders; the coal mine, promising enough in ore but so situated as to be almost unworkable even today, had failed, the Rajah's fortune was exhausted (the Borneo Company later opened a subscription list for him in London with £1,000 and at one time lent him £5,000, demand for the repayment of which led to a certain amount of friction); the Chinese rising had shaken everyone's confidence, and, what with one thing and another, 'the high hopes with which the Company started in 1856 were now brought very low ... As nothing succeeds like success, so nothing failed like failure.'

The next eight years were the making of Sarawak, and both the first and second Rajahs in conversation, in letters, and in public speech, are on record as paying handsome tribute to the Borneo Company. If nothing at first failed like failure, persistence paid in the end, even if, financially, it took about forty years to do so. Organised sailings were begun between Kuching and Singapore, labourers were imported on three-year contracts, and efforts seem to have been made to launch out in any direction that might conceivably pay its way in the end. A sago mill was got going in Muka and the Company advanced money to innumerable families each of whom cultivated their own pepper gardens, no bigger perhaps than an acre and a half but the forerunners of the Sarawak white pepper industry of today.

It was a business of trial and error. In a country covered in forest their thoughts turned naturally to timber, which they hoped to trade with the Company's branches in Calcutta and Hong Kong. The rough-hewn logs were stored afloat in the mouth of the Rejang river to await the ocean carrier and one of the errors was the failure to appreciate that by the time the carrier arrived all the logs except billian wood would be eaten by worms known as 'teredos'. Later, when a saw mill was built at the river mouth, the London office trusted that there would be 'no repetition of this fiasco.' Billian, however, proved teredo-resistant and some of the Borneo Company's billian was used as sleepers for the new Bengal state railways. The antimony workings developed – someone invented an antimony-paint

which was favourably reported upon by Singapore but not heard of again –
but there was in those days no equivalent of the geologist or mining engineer
of today and specimens of every 'find' had to be sent home for analysis by
the Cannon Street smelting works, where recommendations for action
were made, at a range of ten thousand miles and on a purely theoretical
basis, by a Professor Forbes. As time went on, they began to refine the
metal on the spot, in big circular kilns at Busau, and the ingots, bearing the
Company's chop, were sent home to Hallett and Company in London. One
of the originals was for a long time in the Sarawak Museum.

Then there was the great day in September 1867, when Helms, exploring
in the almost uninhabited Bungo mountains near the Dutch boundary,
struggling up a torrent with a party of natives, leaping from boulder to
boulder, came on a huge mass of rock lying across the stream. It had fallen
900 feet from the crag above and was lined with red streaks. The discovery,
he said, in one of those phrases which bring the early days so much to life,
'led very shortly to labours which made the jungle resound to the miner's
blast and the engine's puff.' It was, in fact, quicksilver.

All these were small beginnings but to what extent they were changing
the face of Sarawak was shown in a letter to a Singapore newspaper by
Mr Hugh Low (later Her Majesty's Resident in Perak) in 1868. He had
first arrived in Kuching in 1844 – 'a small Malay village . . . forty miserable
Chinese shops . . . thatched houses . . . not a house of brick in the place, the
only wooden ones those of the Rajah and his officers . . . town in a swamp
surrounded to the house doors by jungle . . . one small schooner communi-
cating with the outside world.'

How different was the picture now! 'I now find it one of the prettiest
places I know in the East. The swamps have been drained by the roads and
the hills are each surmounted by a pretty bungalow . . . A beautiful armed
screw yacht conveys the Government's mandates and officers to the outstations. The *Royalist* keeps up regular communication with Singapore . . .
several ships go annually direct to England with produce collected by the
Borneo Company.' He put the population at 20,000 and – the ultimate
tribute – 'all of them seem to be occupied and happy.'

It was just eleven years since the night that Wellington died.

And now we must bid a reluctant farewell to Helms, without whom we
could not have relived these early days. On 30th May 1872, he left Borneo
for the last time. On his return, it is true, he was involved in a lawsuit with

*Robert Henderson II whose diary brings to life Sarawak and Siam in the 1870s, found the girls of Mukah 'really pretty and celebrated all over Borneo'*

the Company and altogether proved a considerable, if temporary, nuisance, but the lawsuit, having threatened the Company's very existence in Borneo, was settled amicably at home and we may prefer to part company with him as he in turn parts company with Borneo.

'For myself, as I looked at the country for the last time and as the scenes through which I had passed and the work I had done flitted before my mind, I felt satisfied that, though twenty of the best years of my life had been spent in its jungles, they had not been spent in vain.'

*   *   *

Our next witness is Robert Henderson, whom we accompanied to Bangkok. In the same year, 1874, he arrived at Kuching with Professor Robertson, who had been contracted by the Company to give expert opinion on the mineral possibilities of Sarawak. They found the BCL bungalow beautifully placed on a hill beside the river, with a fine garden, 'still neat but they say it misses Mrs Helms,' two beautiful clumps of bamboo on either side, the rooms good, airy, and open, and the Rajah's band playing on the opposite bank. There was also by now a hotel where Robertson's fat assistant, a miner named John Jolly, was accommodated. There was a good deal of gutta in the godowns, some in all shapes boiled by the natives, some in wedge shape boiled by the Company. Miss Burdett Coutts, Henderson noted, had tried sago, sugar, and indigo in the island but had always failed, and had sold out three and a half years previously at a great loss.*

Still, though it was to be twenty years or more before the Sarawak enterprise began paying its way, its feelers were beginning to stretch out to the western world and Henderson observed the *Coraline* loading for England at Pending wharf with oxide below, sulphide above, and rattan canes thick and thin, bad and good. It was August and the captain hoped to be home by January. Students of Sherlock Holmes will prick up their ears on learning that the cargo also included 'Penang lawyers'. The Penang lawyer is a species of stout cane or walking stick and it was the specimen left by Dr Mortimer at 221b Baker Street which set going the story of *The Hound of the Baskervilles*.

Henderson's intended itinerary was to go to Busau (antimony) by boat, thence by tram to Jambusan (antimony), walk to Tegora (cinnabar) and so on to Gading and Gombang. He notes incidentally that the Company at this time were paying £1,000 a year for the sole right to the cinnabar and £2,000 a year for the antimony.

They did the twenty-four miles to Busau in four and a half hours with six men paddling and one steering in the stern – three of these stern-steerers having recently been taken by alligators which, once they acquired the taste, 'preferred man to anything else' – and at Busau they inspected the two antimony furnaces. Next day they walked the ten miles to Tegora Peak to find the BCL bungalow substantial and good but its position absurd, at the top of a hill. Even more absurd, alas, were the splendid engines and stampers which had been installed for processing the quicksilver, having been proved in Austria ten years before to be unsuitable for the purpose. An Austrian expert, Dr Groger, who had been engaged from London, was

*It seems fair to say that this lady, later Baroness Burdett Coutts, was for many years in love with the Rajah and the reverse with the Borneo Company, which she may have regarded as a rival for his attentions. There is no doubt that she had considerable influence on the Rajah in the later days of his rule. Their voluminous correspondence has been collected by Owen Rutter in his book *Rajah Brooke and Baroness Burdett Coutts*.

there at the time. He was unable, he said, to alter his report to the directors and was busy trying to adapt the machinery. They also inspected the old tramway to the peak which had been started two years previously, before they searched well enough to see if there were cinnabar there, and had then been closed up after three months and not used again – 'awful mismanagement.' Nevertheless, they clambered to the top, partly by way of ladders consisting of thin tree trunks with notches for footholds, and celebrated a big dynamite blast on the hillside below with everyone having a gin-and-water on the summit.

Next day they 'batang-walked' to Gading, slithering through the jungle and crossing ravines on the slippery trunks of the batang trees, and arrived at the Company's house, where in the absence of tables or chairs they lay on mats and were bitten to death by mosquitoes. It was here that the Company hoped one day to extract coal and, as they turned in, there was a 'good deal of coal talk,' Professor Robertson relating how he had once descended the 2,400-foot shaft of the Duckinfield deep pit near Manchester in one minute and one second – or just under half-a-mile a minute. As it turned out, they never found coal at Gading, though they did find some cinnabar.

Back in Tegora a wire was waiting in the one-roomed office telling them that the quicksilver was fetching twenty-two pounds per bottle (amount 74 lb.) and the London office would take all they could send. They watched the mercury being separated – the Professor reckoned it superior to that of the best American mines – and then the retorts being emptied of the refuse, mostly sulphur. At this stage the workers were liable to the unpleasant experience known as 'salivation', a loosening of the teeth, and they all had their mouths bound up tightly under the chin. They had learnt by hard experience, for only a year or two previously Helms, on a visit of inspection to the same mine, had had the manager inform him that a Chinaman wished to see him.

'What does he want?' he asked.

'Oh, he's got all his teeth in a bit of paper,' said the manager.

Helms was much shocked but the man apparently did not mind a great deal and a few dollars made him perfectly happy.

It was at Tegora that Henderson was offered a Chinese child, presumably female, by its mother for three dollars, or thirteen shillings at the current rate of exchange. He declined, as did J. B. Cruickshank at Kuching when offered a Dyak bride of surpassing beauty by Dyak standards. Her ears were greatly stretched and had holes in them so large that he actually passed his arm through them.

Back in Kuching the party went up the Sadong river to inspect the coal mine, accompanied by Jolly, another workman named Walters, and the manager, Brodie. The coal looked good and bright, soft and easily worked, and the Professor put it down at two tons per day per man, at which Walters 'said nothing but smiled.' They brought the coal two and a half miles to the landing stage on a wooden tramway in heavy wagons which wore out the rails in a fortnight. Some of the wagons were pushed by Chinamen, two were drawn by buffaloes. This was September and the Company and the Government combined had contracted to supply the Peninsular and Oriental Steam Navigation Company with 300 tons at Singapore by June. They had sent 150 tons and were now going to be hard put to it to supply the rest. The loss was bound to be heavy, Brodie said.

From Kuching they went up to Selantek where there was hope of coal. Through its inaccessibility this came to nothing, but their experience is of interest as showing what the interior of Sarawak was like in the middle seventies, well within the lifetime of many alive today. The first part of the journey was by boat up a narrow river with grass twenty feet high on either side. When their own boat could go no further, they piled their provisions into two small Dyak boats, mere hollowed-out trees, which the Dyaks, when the stream was totally blocked by fallen trees, simply sank and passed under the trees, righting them again on the other side. Finally, they had to get out and walk, sometimes wading up to their middles and harassed perpetually by mosquitoes. Henderson once killed twenty-seven on his ankle at one blow – only to be warned 'not to speak of mosquitoes till he had been to Bangkok.'

On the way they passed a plantation of tapang trees, each with a Dyak ladder of small sticks driven into the trunk and fastened together with rattans. One of them was 120 feet to the first branch. Bees hived at the top of these trees and the Dyaks did quite a trade in beeswax. (The first Borneo Company balance sheet of 1857 includes the item 'Bees wax shipped from Sarawak to Singapore for sale. £663 14s 5d.') Selantek, where a certain amount of out-crop coal was being worked, consisted of Walters' two-room thatched hut and three or four hovels. There had been a small Dyak village but rats had eaten their crops and they had departed starving. Henderson passed the night on the floor with a bundle of Walters' copies of *The*

*The Company's old bridge at Krokong, linking Bau and Bidi mines with outlying deposits*

*Engineer* for a pillow. Next day white ants were in the professor's boxes and a couple of Dyaks turned up merely to look at the 'Orang Puti', or white men. There was one other man in Borneo, they declared, as fat as Jolly. The latter looked supremely miserable and the Professor none too happy, as they were to be left there together. 'It seems almost cruel to leave them,' Henderson recorded, 'but they have made their agreement and we cannot help it.' Robertson's was £500 and all expenses for one year. Jolly's was eighteen pounds a month for three years. They certainly earned their money.

Another expedition took them from Kuching up to Mukah, where they found a half-caste in charge of eight coolies running the sago mill, and the Company advancing money to numerous independent families to grow trees of their own. The local girls caught Henderson's roving eye. He found them 'really pretty, and celebrated all over Borneo.' He also waxed lyrical on the riverside scenery. 'If only we could transfer 200 yards of the wild useless jungle to the banks of the Thames or Mole, what a marvel of beauty it would be thought, with its palms, tree grass, and ferns like trees, with innumerable creepers falling in festoons from branches sometimes 100 feet high.' De Crespigny, in sole charge of the fort at Muka, he found the best Government officer he had seen, but much broken in health. Henderson himself, constantly racked with fever, lived in permanent fear that he might not live to get home.

This phrase, 'much broken in health', recurs persistently in records of the early days and represents perhaps the greatest single difference between the lives of the pioneers, who did not miss radio and refrigerators because they had never heard of them, and the life of the man who serves in the East today. The wastage from sickness was appalling by comparison and it is no surprise to find the Company to have been one of the first subscribers to the London School of Tropical Medicine.

One other expedition, to Talang Talang or 'Turtle Island', may perhaps be mentioned because the island is one of the sights of Sarawak today. Here they watched forty or fifty turtles waddle out of the sea, heave themselves along with their flippers, and lay their eggs in the single patch of deep sand, just as their ancestors had doubtless done for centuries. They rode on the backs of several of them and were duly thrown off. The Rajah used to let the rights to the turtle eggs for £200 a year to a Malay, who, with eggs at about a penny apiece and each turtle laying up to 150 at a sitting, was reckoned to be making a good thing out of it. Today the turtles seem, for a reason unknown, to be dying out. The Government keep a close control on the island to try to preserve them – and the profits from selling the eggs go to the Malay mosques and charities in Sarawak.

★     ★     ★

The middle seventies, the period of Henderson's expedition, were a time of bustling activity and expansion. The Company built a handsome brick office in Kuching to replace the humble edifice in which they had begun, and John Hardie opened a new sago mill at Muka, of which only a forlorn chimney stack bears witness today. The Rajah's vessel, the second *Royalist*, was bought and became the foundation of the Sarawak Steamship Company, and during all this time and for many years to come the Company acted as bankers to the whole of Sarawak. They were the first to be registered as such and for decades arranged for the provision of coinage bearing the image and superscription of the Rajah. With the opening of European banks in the Far East the Company lost the business, but there are still a number of old accounts of Dyak depositors on the books and the Company's cheques are still 'good' as currency in the bazaars all over the country.

In the early eighties the Rajah was inspired to believe that tobacco might profitably be grown in Sarawak and an area near Lundu was duly planted, not without misgivings by the Company. The site at this distance of time seems unaccountable since even today Lundu is reachable only by Dyak paths or by launch from the sea. The venture failed and to the general relief it was the Rajah himself who suggested closing it down. Nevertheless they must have had something to show for their money, since an officer home on leave wrote to the *Sarawak Gazette* to say that he had seen in a shop in Piccadilly boxes of Borneo cigars – the inside label being a coloured view of the waterfront at Kuching, featuring the BCL office and the old Chinese joss house nearby.

Diplomacy was a rough and ready affair in those days by comparison with the present, when the smallest of nations have embassies or legations all over the world. Thus J. W. Edie, the Company's manager in Bangkok, was Norwegian consul-general to Siam while A. R. Malcolm, the present managing director, was vice-consul; St. V. B. Down was Russian vice-consul in Singapore; J. C. Ferrier and A. W. G. Luke were consuls for Siam in Batavia; and Hardie, followed by W. A. Cadell, acted as British vice-consul in Sarawak. This latter appointment lapsed in 1888, the year of the agreement between the Rajah and Queen Victoria's Government whereby the Governor of the Straits Settlements became British agent to Sarawak.

In the eighties the members of the Batavia branch went through an experience which, for all the progress of modern science, would be equally alarming today. Krakatoa is a volcanic island in the Sunda Strait, about 110 miles from Batavia, and on 27th August 1883, it erupted, or it might almost be said exploded, for the second time. The sound was heard in Rodriguez nearly 3,000 miles away, and in South Australia. Dust and stones were hurled seventeen miles into the air and suffused the atmosphere above almost the entire surface of the earth, giving rise to remarkable sunsets as far away as Scandinavia. The sea waves reached Cape Horn, 8,000 miles away, and the sound waves were observed by scientists to pass outwards round the world four times. Meeting each other on the opposite side of the globe, they 'bounced back' to Krakatoa three times and after their fourth

*Family pepper garden in Upper Sarawak with limestone hills in background*

outward journey were lost. Whole islands vanished from sight, others were suddenly created, and altogether 36,000 people lost their lives. W. Lorrain, BCL manager in Batavia, a mere 110 miles away, might reckon himself and his colleagues fortunate not to have been among them. His graphic letter to Cadell, then manager in Singapore, was written on the day after the main eruption and deserves quoting:

'We have been in a dreadful state here since Sunday afternoon owing to the second eruption of Krakatoa, an Island in the Straits of Anjer or rather just outside them, and distant from this about 110 miles. It began with reports like those of heavy Cannon every one of which made the gas lamps in our house tingle, then every five minutes or so there was a louder report which shook everything in the house. We turned in to bed about ten o'clock but at twelve had to get up and open all doors and windows, being afraid of the house falling on us. At one the noise was tremendous and from our verandah we could *see* signs of the disturbance high in the air – we heard the row only too well. We had to stay up – ready to bolt for the open – all night and the row went on just the same when we went to town yesterday morning. When we got to town we found all the natives and Chinese in a state of intense excitement. At ten o'clock it began to get dark, and the darkness gradually increased till twelve o'clock mid-day, when it was really darker than it generally is at that hour of the night. We had had meanwhile heavy showers of ashes and of course all work had to be suspended.

'Then the natives in the office refused to stay with us any longer, as the report came in that the sea was encroaching on the land, and we crossed the road in front of our office and found that the river was running strongly the wrong way, *i.e.* away from the sea inland. In about a quarter of an hour the river which had been very low, was over its banks. Nothing being able to be done as all the natives had bolted, Travers and I at one o'clock shut the office and made a bee line for home. It was pitch dark till we got almost to our door. We found the house, garden, and indeed every place about, covered with about an eighth of an inch of burnt sand. Last night, we had one or two severe shocks every hour or so but today things are much as usual. The concussion of one shock on Sunday night extinguished in a moment every light in the house. I hope it will be quiet tonight as I want a good sleep.'

As a footnote it might be added that until only a few years ago older members of the community in Sarawak used to talk of the 'Malam Pelita' or 'nights of illumination'. According to tradition the ashes falling from Krakatoa, 600 miles away, set fire to some of the low types of jungle on the hilltops and were responsible for the curious burnt-out areas which remain to this day.

*     *     *

The Company takes a certain pride in the fact that a special Act of Parliament was passed for its benefit. Starting with a Deed of Settlement dated 8th May 1856, it was incorporated under the Joint Stock Companies Act of 1856 on 31st October of that year, and until 1890 the Deed of Settlement, amended and altered from time to time, was reckoned to constitute the regulations of the Company. By this time, however, it had been in existence for thirty-six years and was a far different proposition from the infant of the 1850s. The question arose as to whether the numerous alterations had so extended the objects of the Company as to render them unauthorised by the Deed of Settlement. In order to remove the doubts and to define clearly the objects of the Company a Memorandum and Articles of Association were drawn up and duly approved at an Extraordinary General Meeting. Only Parliament, however, could authorise their replacing the original Deed of

Settlement. The 'Borneo Company (Limited) Act 1890' passed through the House of Commons and received the Royal Assent on 14th August 1890.

In the nineties there was a goodish demand for gambier, which is used in tanning and dyeing and as a food seasoning by the Chinese. The leaves are boiled up in great quantity to extract the gambier and it was found that the refuse, if laid a foot deep round the roots, was a splendid manure for pepper vines – all the more acceptable since the most common manure had hitherto been prawn refuse, which the Chinese did not trouble to dig in and which could therefore be detected by more sensitive nostrils a mile away. As a result the Company secured what was known as the Poak Concession – a 20,000-acre strip extending from what is today the Dahan Rubber Estate to Tegora Mountain. For a while, with each family cultivating an acre and a half of pepper and perhaps fifteen acres of gambier with which to manure it, the business was quite a success. Unfortunately the life of a pepper vine is anything up to sixteen years while a gambier only lasts six, so in the end the one failed for lack of the other. The Dahan Rubber Estate, which began with 2,500 acres and was the first rubber to be grown in Sarawak, was planted on part of the Poak Concession and became part of the Sarawak Rubber Estates Limited. Today the Sarawak Rubber Estates, a few miles south-west of Kuching, consist of 2,700 acres, and the Borneo Company still have an active interest in them.

No one can survey Sarawak without casting an ambitious eye on the vast forests of timber with which its surface is mainly clad. The first round of man-versus-forest had been won, hands down, by the forest. In 1904 the Company challenged again. This time they tried buying the logs through Chinese contractors in the interior and floating them down the Rejang on rafts with the tide. They used the unsuitable logs as permanent rafts, floating them up and down time and again, while the suitable ones were hauled ashore, high and dry, at high tide. Altogether the project seemed full of promise. Messrs McDougall and Johnston sent out a modern mill from Lanark accompanied by a Mr McPhee to manage it, but the mill proved more up-to-date than the manager, who turned out to have had little or no experience in this sort of thing. He failed to appreciate that the proposed layout would prove quite unworkable on the site they had chosen and, once erected, the whole mill had to be taken down and put up again elsewhere. The teredos joined in again on the side of the forest; at the same time demand happened to fall off and prices slumped, and, after four years, the

*Sluicing tin ore from mud at Bruseh, Perak*

whole affair had to be abandoned. The mill was dismantled and sent to the Company's branch in Sourabaya: McPhee's bungalow at Rejang was sold to the Sarawak Government and became the assistant district officer's quarters. The forest had won again.

Some years before this the Company persuaded the Rajah to approve the formation of the Sarawak Chamber of Commerce – a circumstance which alone seems to disprove, to the impartial observer of sixty years later, any allegations of monopoly on their part. The original Harvey's son was the first chairman and Mr Ong Tiang Swee was deputy chairman. This particular Chamber lasted only four years, finishing its short life on account of a tendency to dabble in political affairs. It was revived in different circumstances, largely at the Company's instigation, in 1950, to match the activities of separate Chambers of Commerce already formed by the Chinese and Indian communities.

As the present century got into its stride the mineral possibilities of Sarawak could be seen in truer perspective. The antimony was beginning to be worked out and in 1907 the smelting works at Busau closed down, a gigantic ore dump, the accumulation of years, having kept the furnaces going for the final few years. The quicksilver mine at Tegora seems simply to have been abandoned. There are still rails and wheels and bits of machinery lying about, though one of the boilers was sent to the BCL sawmill in Bangkok. Mineral Properties Investigation Limited sent a representative from London to view the workings in 1940 and he reported that there was 'abundant evidence of native mercury all over the place', but it should perhaps be recorded that he never once entered the old workings in the Peaks, the 500-foot mine where the old rails lie. He was, he said, 'allergic to bats'. At any rate nothing more has been done at Tegora and it is now unlikely that anything will. At the turn of the century attention was turning from antimony, quicksilver, and coal to what was to prove for many years the foundations of the Company's fortunes in Sarawak, namely gold.

There is evidence of gold having been worked at Bau, which is five miles north of Tegora, for years before the arrival of the first Rajah. The Chinese were working it in their individual syndicates, or kongsis, when the first European set foot in Borneo, and it was these gold workers, it may be remembered, who were responsible for the rising of 1857. The gold in Borneo occurs in a very fine state and, though by their painstaking personal industry these Chinese made some sort of a living from it, it was not at that time recoverable as an economic proposition for a European company.

Still, gold has always been man's most tempting proposition, and in 1884 the Company bought out the biggest and almost the last of the kongsis, the Shak Lak Mun, and now was out on its own. There were two mines, a mile or two apart, one at Bidi and the other, known as Tai Parit, at Bau. They were of the opencast variety, Bidi going down ninety feet and Bau eventually 250 feet. The Company worked at them for the first few years with quite a degree of success, but clearly the project was not destined to become anything sensational unless some better process could be found for extracting the almost microscopic grains in which the gold occurred. A graphic description of the Bau mine of those days is given by Archdeacon Sharp in his book, previously quoted, *Wings of the Morning*. 'The manager's office is in the midst of the din. Four rough brick walls and a cement floor promise little in the way of luxury. But no one would waste decoration on an office in such a pandemonium of sound while a lingering hope remains of getting away some day from under this resounding roof, where crushers, steam saws, and the clatter of an engineering shop, combined with the rushing of water, make a continuous roar without a moment's cessation.'

The process which was to revolutionise not only Bau and Bidi but mining

*Left, 'punting' along the tramline between the Bau and Bidi gold mines – the only method of transport at the time; and, right, the second Rajah of Sarawak, Sir Charles Johnson Brooke, GCMG, who ruled from 1868 to 1917*

technique in general was discovered by a Glasgow scientist, J. S. McArthur, in the early nineties. The secret lay in the use of cyanide, which dissolves gold more rapidly than any other medium. This discovery, the greatest of its time, completely altered the methods then in use and with the much higher recoveries of precious metals brought new life to the mining world everywhere. The Company got under way with it in Sarawak in 1897 and were the first to adopt it in the Far East.

There are those, incidentally, who still say that in the end the invention of this cyanide process was a mixed blessing. It meant that all eyes were focused on Bau and Bidi when some at least should have been focused elsewhere. In gazing, it is said, on the glittering prospect that seemed to lie ahead in the gold mines, they paid less attention to the more sombre lure of rubber, which in 1908 was beginning to work up to its all-time peak, and of shipping, neither of which were liable in the course of nature to be worked to extinction in the same way. Not that the traditional interest in mining was neglected, apart from the gold. In the early days the Company were closely associated with the Pahang Corporation, for which, as the Pahang Consolidated Company, they still act as agents. The mines at Sungei Lembing, Pahang, are in fact the largest tin lode mines in the world. The present chairman of the Pahang Consolidated Company Limited is D. T. Lewis, who only recently retired from the board of the Borneo Company. He was for many years manager at Singapore, where he was chairman of the Chamber of Commerce and a member of the Legislative and Executive Councils of the old Straits Settlements.

Still, it does seem that the gold, as it has done for many thousands of years past and will doubtless do in the future, did distract eyes which could in the long run have been more profitably turned elsewhere.

In the early days there was no Government control as there is today and all the gold was handled direct by Rothschilds. Government control came in before the first war – during which there was a directive that the Company's gold should be sent for safety to the Mint at Ottawa instead of to London – and has, of course, never been lifted. The Bidi mine closed down about 1910. Whether it was worked out or not is a matter of doubt, but at any rate its monthly output of 600 ounces of fine gold was insufficient to cover costs, with gold at the price of those days. The tailings dump at Bidi must have amounted to close on a million tons. Samples showed an average of two and a half pennyweights per ton, just too little to make treatment of it a paying proposition, and the Company decided to leave it where it was. Later industrious Chinese, some of them old servants of the Company, applied for dumps of ore and formed a number of syndicates. When the price of gold rose, some of them made astonishing profits on a tiny outlay. Bau throughout was the star turn of the two, though its life was clearly limited. In 1923 it had perhaps seven years to go. However, nature stepped in and, with a series of floods unknown previously or since, finished it off. When Tai Parit closed down it had yielded 496,351 ounces of fine gold and had proved itself incomparably the most profitable single venture in Sarawak, both to the Government and the Company. At the prices of those days the gold from Bau brought in something like two-and-a-quarter million pounds. Today it would be worth six million.

There was one man who was primarily responsible for its success – Peter Duguid Thomson. In a saga of a hundred years, in which so many men will have spent their entire working lives in the service of a concern like the Borneo Company, it is impossible to do individual justice to all, but

*Dyak bridge at Krokong. Across this bridge the wives of two members of the staff, with their young children, escaped from the Japanese on Christmas Eve, 1941*

P. D. Thomson deserves more than a passing mention. He must have been a most remarkable man. He was secretary of the Company in 1874, ten years after joining, and became managing director in 1890. He had, of course, been a good deal in the East, but when the cyanide process was being attended by the inevitable teething difficulties he went out again, declaring that he would not return till the thing was a success. He stayed more than a year, working with the men in the mines, with the results already quoted. He was a bachelor and a Scot and with his pointed beard resembled a diminutive edition of King Edward VII. Several senior members of the Company remember him today, all of them with respect and affection. 'You might go into his room as a young junior,' one of them has written, 'to explain that you were not quite sure about something he had asked for. He would get up, pat you on the arm and say in his very quiet Scots accent that there was no need to worry . . . Sometimes he would wander slowly out into the general office, hands clasped behind his back, completely oblivious of his surroundings, but if you were obliged to interrupt him he would never show any ill-temper or impatience and you were invariably met with kindliness and a benign smile. Truly he was a much loved man among the staff of the Borneo Company, and he deserved to be. A typically romantic example of the office boy rising to be the head of his firm – but what a delightfully modest one!' P. D. Thomson, having declared he would quit at sixty, stayed on till he was well over seventy and retired during the first war after more than fifty years of service. It was in keeping with his character that, although a million and a quarter pounds had been paid in dividends during his term of office, he should decline to have his portrait painted for the board room, but, whether he wished it or not, his name is perpetuated in Sarawak – by Thomson Road, which, appropriately enough, links the old Kuching with the new.

Some years after the gold workings closed down at Bau, someone recalled the case of a German prospector called Hundeshagen who was believed to have discovered gold in Sumatra before the first war but had not returned afterwards to pursue the project. The reef he discovered was in the neighbourhood of Balimbing Creek, Bondjol, some thirty or forty miles from Fort de Kock in the Padang highlands. Its precise location nobody knew and to discover it in the close vegetation of an unsurveyed evergreen jungle was no mean task. A number of metal plates fixed to tree trunks gave the first clue, but what turned it into a certainty was the vast stack of beer bottles which had accumulated outside Hundeshagen's original hut and had lain there undisturbed for the best part of twenty years. Though officially known as the Balimbing Concession, the project was henceforward called Bottle Reef by all who worked on it.

When prospecting began in 1928 no one, it appears, ventured to hope that in Bottle Reef they had a second edition of Bau and in the end this judgment proved correct. There was gold at Balimbing but its extraction proved even more difficult than at Bau. Three years were spent in installing and adapting machinery and in 1932 the reef yielded 3,678 ounces, but it was clear even then that its life was going to be short. Next year it produced 3,155 ounces at a considerable profit, but in 1934, as had been forecast, operations ceased and Bottle Reef for the second and probably last time closed down. Whether the next prospector will rediscover it through a stack of Borneo Company beer bottles remains to be seen.

*    *    *

We may now perhaps return to the Siam of the early eighties where the Company are solidly established as the leading overseas merchants and where there occurs an incident which enables the Borneo Company to look with a paternal, though not, one trusts, patronising interest upon another of the greatest trading Companies of the Far East, namely the East Asiatic Company. It was related by H. N. Andersen in his book *Looking Backward*.* Andersen was a Dane who settled ashore in Bangkok at about that time. He became friendly with the foreign minister, who was known universally by the title of his office, 'Kromatah', and was a friendly supporter of European progress. Kromatah appears to have had a finger in pretty well every potentially profitable pie in Bangkok. 'On the East side of the river,' Andersen wrote, 'Kromatah owned a fairly large piece of land, centrally situated in the European business quarter, close to the British and French legations and near the residence of the foreign consuls. This piece of land was in places swampy and in others covered with jungle, but close to the river there were several buildings, including the Oriental Hotel and Møller and Meisners stores, which were both built of teak. I pointed out to Kromatah that with the increasing development this piece of land would become very valuable, if it was cleared and the swamp filled in so that residential houses and business premises could be built on it. If this was done, I should like to rent one of the projected new buildings for the purpose of starting my own business there. I had in mind timber concessions and sawmill business.'

Kromatah proved sympathetic towards this as a joint project but said he would find it difficult to get capital released which he had lent to various firms without causing them financial difficulty. However, he let Andersen select his site and build on it whatever he wished and at the same time gave him power of attorney as manager of the land and permission to exploit it as best he could in their common interest. Andersen settled ashore in the local hotel, which in the absence of a club was the usual meeting place or 'exchange' for the European community, and eventually took it over in

---

*Andersen, who died in 1937, aged eighty-five, became a close friend of King George V and throughout the first world war kept him supplied with information about Germany. In his *King George V* Harold Nicolson notes 'Hans Niels Andersen was a man of influence and wisdom. Born of working class parents, he had served as a cabin boy in a brig trading to the Far East . . . He was the first man to introduce Diesel engines into ships . . . During the war he conducted negotiations with the belligerent governments and was constantly travelling between London, St Petersburg and Berlin . . . King George, as well as the British Foreign Office, held him in high esteem.'

1884, at the same time forming himself into Andersen and Company. He was ready now to tackle the swamp and develop his project if only he could raise the money. It was forthcoming – 40,000 Mexican dollars – from the Borneo Company.

The swamp was cleared and a 1,000-foot road built from the main road to the river, together with the first brick houses built in Bangkok. Kromatah and others added extra capital as time went on and fourteen years later the property was sold – with a profit of half a million ticals, about £25,000, to Kromatah alone. Andersen forged ahead and on these foundations created the East Asiatic Company which is now, with a turnover of millions, one of the biggest and most ubiquitous trading concerns in the world.

Meanwhile our old friend Leonowens has returned to become an honorary cavalry officer – a capacity in which, not surprisingly, we hear no more of him. It was a time when not only Europeans but the Siamese themselves were coming to realise that the vast teak forests of Northern Siam offered brilliant prospects to anyone with the capital, the know-how and, above all, the time to exploit them. Leases for extracting the teak are now, and have been for the past half-century, held by companies, but in the early days individuals took them out in their own name to work on behalf of a company. It was an arrangement slipshod by modern standards and led to a good deal of trouble, notably, in the end, between Leonowens and the Borneo Company, who were both in the business since the beginning. The centre of the teak industry in Siam is Chiengmai, and in the eighties it took six weeks in a pole boat to get there up the river from Bangkok. Except for the spreading of the roads the town itself, with a population of perhaps 30,000 against Bangkok's million, is little changed today, but the journey is a somewhat different proposition. The railway penetrated gradually to Chiengmai, and Germans and Italians were still working on the big tunnel the other side of Lampang when Siam entered the war on the side of the Allies in 1917. Luckily they were stopped at the last moment from blowing it up and today the journey can be done comfortably in twenty-four hours.

For the handful of Europeans who opened up the teak industry, life in Chiengmai was a rough and ready, gay, adventurous business, full of romantic glamour to those of us who survey it from a more orderly and circumscribed world at a distance of seventy years. Wives were not allowed up there in any circumstances, though congenial consolation, it is gathered, was available in other directions, and for a bachelor up to the age of thirty

'There is only one "machine" by which to extract teak from virgin hillsides and float it down the river, and that is our old friend the elephant.' These are working the teak forests of Siam

it was a wonderful life. An assistant marching out from Chiengmai on his elephant might take a fortnight before he reached his work, but he could take with him almost unlimited trappings wherewith to civilise his life in the jungle. Shooting snipe in the paddy fields, and jungle fowl and deer, he could live on the country and, as he sat down to his dinner of roast partridge in his portable chair, could reflect smugly on his opposite number sweltering in Borneo and living on tinned meat and biscuits. He would be working, it is true, during the rainy season and would be soaked to the skin most of the time, but the warmth made it by no means unpleasant. Furthermore the scenery was magnificent – tropical to sub-tropical, with lovely rivers with sandy beds and rocky gorges. In every sense he would be 'out of this world', all on his own apart from native labour for three months or more, with a capital time waiting for him in Chiengmai when he got back – tennis, squash, golf (flat, rather uninteresting, but laid out for nothing by the best architects from home through a correspondence in *The Field*!), and polo on the ponies which he kept in any case for his work. Despite which, when a man had been out for three months and had acclimatised himself to a life which suits some people's temperament so well, it was often difficult to get him back at all.

The early teak leases were taken up direct from the ruling prince, the Chao Luang of Chiengmai. The Laos tribe, like a good many others before Siam became a closely-knit country, owed allegiance to the King but were virtually autonomous. Leonowens got leases on behalf of the Company, whose manager he was, but in his own name. The Chao himself was a splendid character, his star turn being his ceremonial dance with candles on the head of an elephant. He and Leonowens got on like a house on fire, except once when they met in the jungle and it was observed that Leonowens was accompanied by a greater number of elephants than the Chao, an incident which involved loss of face to the latter and led to representations on a diplomatic level. The Chao was a great gambler and almost every evening Leonowens would be rowed across to the palace to play with him, fortified by the knowledge that losses could be paid from the Company's petty cash, while winnings could be regarded among the perquisites of his office. His assistant, Macfie, another of the 'characters' who so liberally besprinkle the pages of any story like that of the Borneo Company, being only a junior, had to swim the river. He was met on the other side by the Chao's servants with towels and a pair of Chinese pants. The main disadvantage of being a junior was, however, the fact that he had to gamble with his own money.

Leonowens spent eleven years in the Company's service. A boat for up-river teak work was named after him, the *Captain Leonowens*, and when his wife died in 1893 the Company made him a grant and enabled him to send his children to Canada, but a year or two later dark suggestions emerged at more than one board meeting that he was 'trading on his own'. Friendly hints were passed on by the Company's rivals, the Bombay-Burmah Trading Company, that their manager was . . . 'well, not quite . . .' Eventually the break came, whereupon Leonowens, keeping some of the original teak leases for himself, joined Bombay-Burmah – an episode which doubtless led to bitter gnashing of teeth at the time but at which one can hardly help smiling now – more especially as the Borneo Company, Bombay-Burmah, and the firm which Leonowens himself founded later and which bears his name, Louis T. Leonowens Limited, find themselves drawn into ever closer association by common interests today. Nevertheless, Leonowens played a personal part in founding the great teak industry of Siam, as surely as his more celebrated mother played a part in influencing the two men who turned Siam into the country it is today.

Teak has dominated the BCL story in Siam continuously for eighty years. To the outsider the extraction of some of the heaviest timber in the world from the virgin forests of Upper Siam may appeal almost as a romantic saga. Those who spend their lives at it may be forgiven for regarding it more as a matter of capital, patience and perspiration. From the time that they ring-bark or 'girdle' a tree high up in the forest to the time it reaches Bangkok can never be less than five years, and may well be more. They have to wait three years for it to die, since green teak will not float. Then they have to get it from the hillside down to the nearest creek; from the creek, during the rainy season, to the side river; from the side river to the nearest main river, the Me Ping or Me Wang; and thence down to Bangkok.

The logs float down free as far as Raheng – each one hammer-marked all over with the owner's mark* – and in the big storage grounds they are sorted out, assembled into rafts, and floated down the river, the whole operation controlled by a couple of men per raft who spend their entire day

---

* A fact which has not prevented teak-stealing from being a highly profitable industry in rural Siam, where whole villages assemble to drag logs from the river. The courthouse at Chiengmai is full of teak from unidentifiable sources.

in the water, controlling the rafts with long spade-like wooden poles attached to ropes and incidentally carrying their cigarettes on their heads under felt hats. At night they anchor up and camp in thatched cabins on the rafts. Before the war the Company had its own sawmill in Bangkok but unhappily this was looted during the war. The Bombay-Burmah mill survived and for a while they shared it with BCL and the Anglo-Thai Corporation, but all BCL teak is now sold in the rough.

Sometimes, as before the first war, handsome profits have been made. At other times slumps in other parts of the world have caused teak to fetch half the price it would have fetched when first the tree was girdled. Everyone operating in Siam, whether with British capital or not, was hard hit, for instance, by Empire Preference in favour of teak from India and Burma – in 1933 Siam's exports had fallen to sixty-five per cent in two years through tariff barriers which no one could have anticipated either when the leases were signed and the government royalty agreed upon or for that matter when the logs that came on the market in 1933 were girdled in 1927. And in 1933 neither the directors of the Company nor the men in the forests could be expected to know that, while the economic slump would be over, buyers in 1938 would only be purchasing from hand to mouth through fear of war.

★     ★     ★

Despite the fantastic excavators, caterpillars, bulldozers, and such like that were produced by the war, there is virtually only one 'machine' with which to extract teak from virgin hillsides, and that is our old friend the elephant. All mankind, irrespective of age or race, is fascinated by the elephant, and the more you work with them, so those with experience will tell you, the greater grows the fascination. Readers of *Elephant Bill*, by Colonel J. H. Williams, who has more than once been consulted by the Borneo Company, will appreciate their sentiments. Anywhere a man can go an elephant can go, through narrow jungle tracks or along precipitous mountain paths which no machine can reach. His life cycle, too, is the same as that of a man. He is broken in at the age of four, goes to school to learn his job till he is seventeen, and is at his muscular peak between thirty and forty. Thereafter his age and experience make him immensely valuable till, at the age of sixty, he retires. Sensibly enough, he starts work at dawn and stops at about two o'clock, declining to work through the heat of the day. He takes every third day off, and in the dry weather from January till May retires altogether to a rest camp higher up in the hills where there is green fodder. Each working elephant is attended by a mahout and a foot-man, and the occasional savage one is also accompanied by a spearman whose job is to hold his spearpoint within a few inches of the beast's beady little eye. A spearman is also called upon when one of them goes 'musth', which means that he is seeking female company. This is reckoned some-what bad management since it can generally be avoided, as in army camps during the war, by keeping the creature fully occupied. While the herd must in the course of nature be maintained, the business, if not kept in check, can be a costly one, since nature in this case takes two years and a further female elephant inevitably downs tools and attaches itself to the mother and child as a kind of 'auntie'.

As a teak tree is knotty and has a varying heart liable to twists and turns inside the trunk, a long straight plank is a rarity and they will go to any lengths to get a sound thirty-foot log out whole. It is here that the elephant comes into his own, not merely for sheer strength but for his adaptability and the wisdom that comes from forty years in the forest. It is true that the mahout puts him into position, but if the elephant doesn't know that the teak is destined for a sawmill in Bangkok he certainly knows what is to be done with it now, and the best, possibly the only, way of doing it. The Company in the late nineties maintained a stud of 600 – there are perhaps fifty or sixty now, with some hundreds hired from contractors during the season – and many are the tales of their sagacity. Sometimes whole stacks of logs, not yet assembled into rafts, get piled up in the river and the only thing – perhaps one should say the only person – who can untangle them is an experienced elephant. Logs are like trusses of hay on top of a stack, or matches in the 'match game' – there is always one which will come away without disturbing the rest. The elephant has to stand downstream of the log-stack, dislodging them one by one, and every time the right one. He knows as well as anyone else that if he disturbs the stack in the wrong way he will have several hundred tons of teak smashing down on him in mid-river.

Of the many stories they will tell you of elephants and their ways, and it is a subject to which the layman can sit up listening all night, perhaps the most appealing is of the one which tried to cross the river while hobbled by a chain on the forelegs and got the chain – which is designed to stop them

*Floating teak down to Bangkok; the Company's boats in the Me Ping rapids*

roving too far in search of fodder – inextricably entangled in the branch of a sunken log. The river was rising fast and by the time help could be summoned he had disappeared under water. Mahouts dived frantically to release the chain, to no avail. Another elephant was brought along, also to no avail. Eventually they managed to attach a very long chain and wire ropes. In the meantime, twice every minute, up came the elephant's trunk like a periscope. Finally, with much heaving of other elephants from the bank, the branch of the log was broken and the beast was freed. He had been in the water for sixteen hours, for most of the time totally submerged and breathing through his 'snorkel'. And at no time during all the prodding and diving and heaving did he show the least sign of panic or interfere with the proceedings in any way.

The outside observer, surveying the Company's hundred years in Siam in a cheerfully detached sort of way, may be forgiven for concluding that the red-letter day in all this long and honourable record was founded upon an achievement not by any particularly gifted or hardworking member of the staff, but by the Company's elephant who gave birth, one day in 1926, to a white baby. Readers of 'Anna' may remember the sensation caused by the discovery of a white elephant in the annual round-up near Ayuthia, when seventy-five royal barges and a hundred boats were at once ordered to take the King and his suite to the scene. It is a tenet of the Buddhist religion, and one which we may respect since so many secretly subscribe to it in Christian countries, that the spirits of the departed return to earth in other forms – and indeed that the Great Buddha himself from time to time does so. Those especially worthy return as birds or animals of pure white, and of these the rarest and most distinguished is the white elephant.

It fell to D. F. Macfie, now forest manager in Siam – more than thirty years since the days when he used to swim across to gamble with the Chao – to do the honours regarding the new phenomenon. Pictures and accounts of it appeared in newspapers and magazines all over the world. To the sensation it caused in Siam his own accounts give graphic witness:

'We have had a hectic week of it over this White Elephant Calf which has been born to one of the BCL elephants. It was born last May, and rumours at once spread that it was a real white elephant and had all the proper points for a white elephant to have, light red skin, white hair on head and body, light blue eyes, and a very white roof to its mouth. The authorities heard of it and so, at the request of the Chief of Chiengmai and the Siamese commissioner here, I had it brought in, when they at once both went in off the deep end about it, and said it was a true white elephant, and an incarnation of Buddha, and very sacred and holy. Wherever it went it was followed about by hundreds of people who knelt to it and worshipped it, and fed the mother on cakes and sugar cane till she nearly got ill herself. It was escorted in by about seventeen big tuskers, and a band and gongs, across the bridge (where elephants are not allowed to cross as a rule, but this one was much too holy to be asked to ford the river), and so to the BCL compound. The poor little animal was wonderfully good and stood by its mother scratching one hind leg with the other, looking very bored with the proceedings. I went out after dinner at about 10 pm, to see how it was getting on and found it sleeping peacefully between its mother's forelegs, while she was still munching sugar-cane.'

Macfie recorded that it proved to be an extraordinarily quiet, nice little animal, not a bit pugnacious or mischievous like other baby elephants. Everybody attributed this to the fact that it was a reincarnation of Buddha, and all sorts of stories were circulated, such as that when it was taken down to the river to bathe it always bathed up stream of its mother, and always chose slightly higher ground to sleep on. So great was the crowd that

Macfie decided to bath it in the compound, for which purpose he produced a huge zinc footbath. The little beast promptly got right inside the bath and sat down – 'the most comical sight you ever saw' – and this again was taken as proof of its human or god-like incarnation.

The whole thing was considered the most wonderfully lucky occurrence as, in the year that King Chulalongkorn acceded to the throne of Siam, this same Chief of Chiengmai's father had a white elephant calf born in Chiengmai which he presented to the King – and the King reigned for a record period of forty years. Now, in the first year of the new King's reign, this white calf was born in Chiengmai – an indisputable omen of prosperity. The King decided to come up to Chiengmai in January, the first time any King of Siam had ever been up there, and altogether the Borneo Company were reckoned to have acquired much merit. The visit was a tremendous success. The King and Queen were met at the station and escorted through the city by eighty-seven of the biggest elephants in Siam, and liked the place so much that they announced their intention of building a residence there and turning Chiengmai into a kind of Siamese Balmoral.

Macfie presented Their Majesties with an album of photographs and made a short address in which he said, 'It is a matter of the keenest gratification to the Borneo Company Limited, and especially to the staff employed in working the royal teak forests in northern Siam, that in the seventy-first year of the Company's career in Siam, and in the first year of Your Majesty's reign, it should have happened that an elephant portending prosperity both to Your Majesties and to your Kingdom, should so opportunely have been born.'

The King in turn said he was extremely pleased with the elephant, which he thought was a very good specimen of a true white elephant, and, in thanking the Company for it, he wished them many years of prosperity in Siam.

Eventually the time came to take the now Sacred Elephant and its mother down to Bangkok, a journey of some six days, in a special truck with electric light, four water showers, and a telephone attachment through to the engine. The little creature, not unnaturally, declined at first to get in, so they sent for a big tusker who bundled it in willy-nilly seated on its posterior protesting violently. One of the mahouts who was shut up in the truck with it to ride on its neck and keep it calm, got his foot caught in one of the chains and nearly lost his leg, but eventually the journey was over, and it

*Phra Sawet Kohadejdilok, the white elephant, and his mother*

arrived amid unprecedented scenes in Bangkok. 'The Siamese,' reported Macfie, 'went absolutely mad over it and there have never been such scenes – people being crushed to death in the crowds, or pushed into the canals and drowned.'

An enclosure was erected for the elephant and its mother in front of the royal palace, and for days on end people flooded in from every quarter of Siam to witness a rite which had not been held within the last forty years. Macfie and other officials of the Company including the present managing director, A. R. Malcolm, attended at 9 am in full evening dress – which is the ceremonial dress in Siam as in the Vatican, though one difficult to bear in the full day-time heat of the tropics – and Macfie was presented by the King with the Order of the White Elephant and a gold bowl with a Siamese inscription giving the King's name in full as follows – 'Prabat Somdech Paramindra Maha Prajadhipok Phra Pok-Klao Chaoyuhua Siam.'

The feasting appears to have gone on all day and all night for the best part of a week. 'I hope,' wrote Macfie in closing his account, 'for the sake of my successors that no BCL elephant so far forgets itself in future as to have a white baby.'

The end of the story, though a trifle sad, may perhaps be added. Poor Phra Sawet Kojadejdilok, as the elephant was called, died on 19th January 1943. He was then just eighteen years old. His carcase was handed to the animal welfare department and his skeleton kept for educational purposes. Perhaps because of the war, perhaps because times and beliefs change, he was given no ceremonial funeral.

★    ★    ★

The first world war made an impact upon the Company which no doubt was thought considerable at the time but which now, by comparing it with the second, can be seen in different perspective. The first war did not really hit the Far East. Looking back over the forty intervening years, one suspects that its main impact came afterwards. It was a volunteers' war and in every body of men gathering together when it was over, there was a permanent if unspoken rift between those who had joined up and those who had not. As usual, much injustice, perhaps unwittingly, was done to some of the latter, many of whom tried to join and were turned down, while others were manifestly making a greater contribution by staying where they were. In August 1914 the Borneo Company, like any other reputable concern, decided on allowances of pay and a guarantee of re-employment to members of the staff who joined up. Some, whose names appear in the Roll of Honour on page 119, lost their lives in the fighting. A. H. Evans, manager of the Alexandra Brickworks in Singapore, was killed during a mutiny among the Indian troops there, while F. Hilton, a departmental manager in Singapore, was torpedoed and drowned on his way back there from home. B. de F. Garland, acting manager in Batavia, was captured by the German raider *Wolf* and interned for some months but survived to return to his post.

The fearful casualties of the first war left the younger men who survived it with a feeling of what may charitably be called light-hearted relief. They were alive when they had not expected to be and nothing much else seemed to matter. It was in this spirit that post-war juniors at home enlisted to seek their fortune with the Company in the Straits Settlements, Sarawak, Java, and Siam. Some of them stayed on and now adorn positions of eminence in the boardroom. Some lasted a few months; some, on landing, were persuaded to take the same boat home; and one or two set out and never got there at all.

For many years, beginning before the first war and ending with the Bolshevik revolution, the Company had acted as agents to the Russian Volunteer Fleet. This was a state-owned concern belonging to the Imperial Russian Government and in many ways was not dissimilar to the British Royal Naval Reserve. Most of its officers had served in the Russian navy, while the ships flew the Russian ensign with a special insignia and in the event of war could with little delay be turned into armed merchantmen. Some of the vessels were armed during the Russo-Japanese war. In peace time they ran a regular service from Vladivostok down the Japanese and Chinese coasts to Singapore and thence to Odessa via Colombo and Port Said. From Odessa they carried on a substantial pilgrim trade to Jedda and in 1914 decided to enter the same line of business from Singapore to Jedda with a ship called the *Ekaterinaslav*. After many hold-ups to bring this ancient vessel into line with British and Straits Settlements regulations she sailed for Jedda with a full load of pilgrims and was just entering the Red Sea when war broke out. Despite enemy vessels in the vicinity she made port safely with her pious cargo. At the same time the Company were acting as agents not only for the Russo-Asiatic Bank but also the Northern Steamship Company of Russia which also ran regular services from Vladivostok to Europe. It was for their services to the Russian Volunteer Fleet, however, that in 1915 N. A. Rospopoff, the Russian consul-general in Singapore, presented J. Denniston, the Singapore manager, with the unique gold-enamelled wine jug which he in turn bequeathed to the Company and which now adorns the boardroom.

'His Imperial Majesty, my august sovereign, having graciously accepted my report and acknowledged the friendly services to this consulate by you as manager of the local branch of the Borneo Company,' wrote Mr Rospopoff, 'was pleased to present you with a gold enamelled wine jug, in old Russian style. While handing to you this gracious mark of His Majesty's personal attention, I am glad to join to it the renewed expression of my thanks for the highly appreciated good services and kindness always displayed towards this consulate by the staff of the Borneo Company Limited at Singapore.'

Alas, the story ended on a less happy note. The Company were doubtless

*Gold enamelled wine jug presented by the late Czar of Russia for the Company's services to the Russian Volunteer Fleet*

delighted with the wine jug but would have been even more delighted with the eighty thousand odd pounds owed them on the Russian Volunteer Fleet's account when the Bolsheviks repudiated all the debts owed by the Czar's Government. Negotiations dragged on for several years and in the end they had to settle in 1923 for £6,998.

Around the turn of the century the Company went into two commodities, if such they may be called – one of them almost as old as man, the other destined completely to change his way of life, namely bricks and motors. In 1899 BCL bought some Chinese brickworks in the Pasir Panjang district, four or five miles from the centre of Singapore, where they installed new machinery and laid the foundations of what was to be, after a certain number of ups and downs, a profitable venture. In 1927 further brickworks were opened in Butterworth – they were sold four years ago on account of transport difficulties between Butterworth and Penang – and in 1928 the original venture was floated as a public company registered in Singapore with a capital of 1,400,000 Straits dollars and the name of Alexandra Brickworks. Today the works can produce a million and a half bricks a month and countless millions of their bricks have gone towards the building of modern Singapore.

Four years ago, for the first time in their history, the Company launched out from their ancient and traditional territory in the East, and bought and modernised a brick and tile works in Edmonton, Alberta – an action that would have severely shaken the editor of the *Hong Kong Times* who wrote so critically in 1858 of a concern called the Borneo Company presuming to trade so far afield as Siam. The Canadian concern, whose title is Alexandra Brick and Tile Company (Canada) Limited, has had the usual teething troubles for a couple of years but has now started to produce bricks. Coupled with it is a concrete blockmaking business, which may in the end prove the more significant of the two. Concrete blocks, simple to manipulate by comparison with bricks, are finding increasing favour in the wave of building which is going on, and is likely to be intensified, in Canada.

As for the motor cars, the Company had been flourishing for the best part of half a century before the first motor car turned up in Malaya. They were in the motor business from the start, supplying the more enterprising citizens with these new-fangled engines of destruction, despite the existence of hardly a mile of road really suitable for their use, but as the internal combustion engine began to revolutionise the daily life of the civilised world, especially after the first war, the business grew to such proportions that the motor section was floated off in 1925 to become one of the most persistently successful of the Company's subsidiaries, namely Borneo Motors Limited.

Those who are old enough will always look back on the twenties as the golden age of motoring. Driving was still an art and the man who knew what was going on under the bonnet still scored over the man who did not. What sold motor cars in the early days was enthusiasm, and the pioneers of Borneo Motors certainly had it. None more so than the first managing director, the late Claud Jackson, whose son, incidentally, entered the Company's service in 1955. Jackson's Straker-Squire was the first car in Malaya to be fitted with a disappearing hood and the first to be sprayed with the new iridescent paint, as against painting by hand. He organised hill climbs, speed trials, and the first 'round the island' race, in which the competitors seem to have spent much of their time pulling each other out of

The 'golden age of motoring': the late Claud Jackson of Borneo Motors in the 'Round the Island' race, Singapore; and (below) the Chevrolet climbing the 2000-foot bridle path on Kladang mountain, Ipoh

*A hazard of the jungle. Python caught at Miri, Sarawak. Its meal was a whole wild boar*

muddy ditches. He also motorised and fitted with electric light a Chinese junk which he bought from an Australian who intended to sail it to England but, after floating sideways as far as Penang, abandoned it. In this strange craft he gained much face by visiting ships of the Royal Navy.

They must have been a happy band of warriors, though too many of their names, alas, appear now on the Roll of Honour. Many of them stripped their cars and produced them in completely redesigned versions of their own. Bellingham-Smith, probably the best mechanic in Malaya, was one. After serving as second in command of a volunteer armoured car unit, he died in Siam. Geoffrey Maund, whose brother commanded the *Ark Royal* when she was sunk, was the earliest of the Austin Seven experts. He died as a prisoner of war. Crowther-Smith, later killed in the war, was a guiding genius behind the Johore grand prix, in which he distinguished himself by pitching personally, unhurt, into the grandstand, while a Chinese driver just behind ran upon his wrecked motor car and found himself perched on the wreckage, still driving but now motionless. Another was Pat Atkins, a first war pilot who came back to fly in the second, and ferried admirals and air marshals at the last moment from Singapore to a neighbouring island, where almost the entire party succumbed in an episode which was later mentioned by Sir Winston Churchill in his memoirs. It was Atkins who, in the twenties, took a Chevrolet up a 2,000-foot bridle path on Kladang mountain near Ipoh, levering and manhandling it round the corners. He cabled the manager in Penang saying 'Chevrolet climbs 2,000-foot peak' and received the answer 'Why?' Atkins replied 'To get to the top.'

In 1926 N. G. Reddish and A. O. Marshall sealed a Chevrolet in top gear and drove it, complete with a reporter from the *Penang Gazette*, 500 miles over the passes from Penang to Singapore, where it was duly exhibited by Borneo Motors. Ten years later Reddish drove another Chevrolet over the same road in just over ten hours, an average of fifty miles an hour, including stops at interstate customs which no longer exist. This record was attacked many times but it was nearly twenty years before it was broken.

These extra-curricular activities may perhaps be said to represent the more flippant side of the serious business of buying and selling motor cars, but they represent too an enthusiasm which laid the foundations of a business which does more than a third of the entire motor trade in Malaya today.

*     *     *

For more than thirty years the Company has been growing tea in Sumatra, with varying fortune, through its subsidiary, the Haboko Tea Company. A year or two after the end of the first war the Chairman was reporting the usual difficulties of opening up new areas, a heavy fall in tea prices eighteen months before, and altogether 'little of an optimistic nature.' Nevertheless the estate was described by Roger Bannerman, who had been sent to inspect it, as 'a property of great value and one with a very sound future before it.' In 1923 the tea industry took a sudden and notable turn for the better and the estate showed its first profit. For the next three years things continued to go well, each crop being advantageously sold a year or so in advance, and in 1929 the crop totalled over a million pounds – at an average cost of production which to the younger housewife of today may seem like something out of another world, as indeed in many ways it was, namely 8·324 pence per pound.

In the meantime it was decided gradually to open up 3,500 acres of the estate with rubber, the whole of it with luck to be completed by 1931. The ancient factory was replaced with a modern building and the rubber development was probably on as modern lines as any in existence, though the general agreement on rubber restriction limited the crop to just under one million pounds. On the whole both the rubber and the tea seemed to be set reasonably fair, when the slump of the early thirties came to undo most of the hard work of the years since the war.

The fortunes of the tea and rubber ventures in the Dutch East Indies followed a pattern that was common to commercial concerns all over the Far East – perhaps, though that is a wider subject, all over the world. Small booms were followed by small slumps, the whole culminating in the world-wide slump of the late twenties, then gradually recovering in time for the second war.

So far as the Borneo Company was concerned, 1923 was a turning point after three thoroughly lean years, and in the following year every department was covering expenses or making a profit. A fine new office went up in Bangkok, shares were taken in the new Sungei Kinta Tin Dredging Company, and the office building in London was sold, the Company becoming tenants so that the capital could be more profitably employed in the Far East than in city property.

The first chill draught was the sudden removal of restriction on the export of rubber, 'the method chosen for announcing which,' declared the Chairman, 'could not have been better calculated to destroy confidence.' Low prices for all the principal commodities in the Company's territories meant that customers had little or nothing to spend. The only exception was teak, but here the principal markets, India and China, were bedevilled by political upheavals, to say nothing of the fall in silver. In London in 1931 A. G. A. Jamieson, retiring as Chairman, observed, 'I wish that the occasion could have been a more auspicious one and that I could have sung my swansong on a different note.' It was impossible, he said, to make profits at the present level of commodity prices, however drastic the economies might be; impossible indeed to avoid a heavy loss in the ordinary course of business. In the course of the next two or three years economies were indeed drastic. Everyone, including directors, had their remuneration cut; costs in the East were reduced by thirty-six per cent and in London by forty-six per cent and were now reckoned at rock bottom. No one could earn profits in teak, tea or rubber, more especially rubber, which in 1932 sank to its all-time low of just under a penny three farthings a pound, landed in London. And to think that it had once, in 1910, fetched 12s 9d. Soon in Java and Sumatra surplus cash and credit had virtually disappeared. What with this and the awkwardness, to say the least of it, of the trading conditions imposed by the Dutch, there was nothing for it but to close down the imports business in those countries, cut the losses – they ran well into six figures – and abandon this branch of the business.

The turning point in what would now be politely called a 'recession' was 1934. Things suddenly, almost unaccountably, got better, at least in Malaya and Sarawak, though in Siam rice and timber prices had further still to fall. In Malaya it was thought prudent to add to the staff again and a new spirit suffused operations in the Far East. 'The old days,' said the Chairman in his report for 1935, 'when the British merchant could sit in his office and deal with his buyers through intermediaries are gone, as also are the days when the British manufacturer could dictate as to what was best suited for the market. If we are to be able to trade successfully, it is essential to study the requirements of the market ahead, and to maintain direct and personal touch with buyers. This policy has been the foundation of the success of Japan in the past and we may well take a leaf out of her book.'

This was the year, incidentally, of the great pepper crash in London, in which the Company, the Chairman added, 'though Sarawak has the at present somewhat unenviable distinction of being the principal pepper-producing country in the Empire, was in no way involved.'*

In the meantime, though the Haboko tea was giving rise to a certain amount of anxiety, the rubber was coming along splendidly. The estate was carefully managed by Harrisons and Crosfield Limited, and, again to quote the chairman, 'the present health and strength of the trees I saw four years

---

*Pepper is sold in two forms, white and black. A number of gentlemen in the City of London were inspired to corner the world supply of white pepper. Their knowledge of this commodity did not, however, run to an appreciation of the fact that white pepper is only black pepper in another form and that the supply would therefore be virtually unlimited. Their downfall brought unmerited losses to many respectable city firms, including some that drew their origins from among the earliest members of the Borneo Company.

*The Magazine Road godown where two of the Company's staff destroyed 36,000 bottles of liquor to prevent them falling into the hands of Japanese*

ago as striplings was extraordinary.' The quota was being disposed of advantageously under the international rubber restriction schemes and in three years' time, he thought, the estate would compare favourably with any in the East.

The next two years saw first 'very appreciable improvement' and then 'an unexpected and abnormal rise in all commodities.' Everything seemed set fair again and 1938 got off to a tremendous start. Alas, it flattered to deceive. A year that started apparently without a cloud on the horizon ended with a slump more severe even than 1931–33. Perhaps the most serious repercussions to anyone trading in Malaya were due to the huge sums being squeezed from the Chinese there to support the war between China and Japan.

Back in Sarawak, however, the Company had been skirmishing for a further tilt at the forest and had secured permission from the Rajah to extract timber from a large area of virgin territory. A couple of elephants were sent over from Siam as an experiment – it was before their export was prohibited from that country – and they seemed to be thriving well, though one of them was to die in 1940. An expert was sent to survey the Phillipines and British North Borneo as well as Sarawak and in due course, on his putting in a favourable report, the Company launched the venture 'The Rejang Timber Concession' with a forest headquarters at the foot of the Pelagus Rapids and a sawmill at Salim. The hazards of working the forest in the interior of Borneo were still considerable, the most persistent being the ambrosia beetle, which attacks the living tree the moment it is felled and barked, and the rapids. Apart from all this, European markets proved none too fond of the hardwoods and semi-hardwoods of Sarawak, and though strenuous efforts were made both then and after the war to sell them elsewhere, the venture on the upper reaches of the river closed down and the Company retired to prepared positions in the swampy area round the delta, there to extract Ramin timber through a subsidiary, the Austral Timber Company, which is at the moment successfully sending it to Europe, Australia, Africa and Hong Kong. The forest had not this time, as in the first two contests, won by a knock-out – but it could still be said to be well ahead on points.

*    *    *

If the first war made little impact on the Company, the second for three and a half years completely extinguished it. For some years the Japanese had been infiltrating into Siam and Malaya as photographers, barbers, and such like and it was clear even in 1939 that, when they did come into the war, Siam was almost certain to fall to them. The British authorities there were able to take action which, for reasons of morale, they were unable to take in Malaya, and requested that all wives and families be evacuated from Siam. This was to a large extent done, but during the 'silent' period in the Far East coinciding with the 'phoney' war in Europe, many of them drifted back. Business went on very much as usual and, encouraged by big American purchases, tin and rubber in Malaya especially thrived. Then on

8th December 1941, the Japanese launched the first air attack on Singapore and within a matter of days they were in Bangkok, arriving almost without warning on lorries specially adapted to run on railway lines. The Siamese resisted them genuinely enough, particularly in the south, but all was over in a matter of days. The Japanese at once commandeered the BCL office as their transport headquarters; European civilians were picked up either by them or the Siamese, and in due course the whole of the Company's staff in Bangkok found themselves interned, with 400 others, in the University of Moral and Political Sciences beside the river bank. Here in a compound about 200 yards by seventy, they were interned for nearly four years. Among them was K. H. Simpson, manager in Singapore, who had had the good fortune, hardly to be realised as such at the time, to have been sent up with the food controller for Singapore to organise the supply of rice from Siam, and so to be caught in Bangkok instead of Singapore.

Those who were interned for those weary years in Bangkok are the first to emphasise that their lot was not an unhappy one by comparison with those who were taken in Singapore. They go on record as saying that the behaviour of the Japanese in Bangkok was exemplary and that the Siamese on the whole, though they declared war on the Allies, rarely wavered in their belief in an Allied victory. The lot of the internees was made none the easier, however, by the numerous repatriation schemes, in none of which their turn ever seemed to come. Apart from Simpson and N. J. Davies and his wife, who were repatriated on medical grounds, the rest of the Company's staff were left to the bitter end – mainly, as it later turned out, through the refusal of the Australians to repatriate Japanese pearl fishers.

As time went on, the Japanese brought numerous British prisoners of war to Siam to build the notorious railway to Burma. These men were desperately in need of money, drugs, and news, and, in providing them, often at great personal risk, the Company's internees were able to feel that they were doing something really worth while. The amount of money and drugs smuggled through to the prisoners was incredible and for the leading part he played in these exploits Peter Heath received the OBE. Another member of the Company's staff, Albert Tanner, who was not interned, being Swiss, and a Siamese, Nai John Aribarg, also risked their lives to help the British prisoners and Tanner was not only awarded the OBE, but – an unusual action on the part of the Swiss Government – was allowed to accept it.

Incidentally, every penny on which internees had pledged credit was repaid after the war.

In the north most of the Company's staff were able to get away, though many of them had to walk the best part of 150 miles to Burma in order to do it and in one or two instances, when Burma was attacked, had to walk back again. It was on those in Singapore and Sarawak that the full horror fell – but before it did so there occurred an episode which those of the Company who took part in it may for ever look back upon with pained regret. In the Company's godown in Magazine Road were 36,000 bottles of assorted brandy, whiskey and gin, not to mention champagne, on which duty, alas, had already been paid. The authorities, suspecting that, while the Japanese were insufferable enough when sober, they would be a great deal worse when intoxicated, ordained the destruction of the entire stock. The denial party consisted of T. C. Martine and J. Bennett who started by tipping the stock case by case through a hole to the floor below. Later, as the pile of 'empties' grew, they tried throwing individual bottles against the wall. This was effective but would have taken them upwards of a week to complete. They were, after all, almost certainly the only two men in history who have attempted to destroy £30,000 worth of spirits single-handed.

The work went on all through the day and they had almost finished when a Japanese shell pitched through the roof and they left in a hurry, the whole sorry scene illuminated by the soap factory blazing nearby and £30,000 now literally 'down the drain'.

The Japanese had expected to find 500 Europeans, other than troops, in Singapore. Instead they found 4,600. The whole community were summoned to the Cricket Club ground and, after standing for a day in the sun, were marched first to temporary camps and then thirteen miles to Changi prison, where they were put into accommodation designed for 600 criminals. To the Japanese they rated lower even than prisoners of war. Here for two years of their internment they lived in grossly overcrowded and primitive conditions, lorry-loads from time to time being taken away in the small hours of the morning by the Gestapo, or Kempetai, for questioning about alleged illicit radios and such like, and often not being returned. Unlike those who were held in Bangkok they had no access to money except what could be smuggled in. This was an operation which cost a number of internees their lives – among them, very nearly, the Bishop of Singapore, the Rt Rev Leonard Wilson, who is now Bishop of Birmingham.

The dominant fear, though, particularly among those married internees who were unfortunate enough to have their families segregated in the women's block of the gaol, was that any trifling misdemeanour in the men's part of the camp would result in some punishment being inflicted on the women.

In Borneo the situation was also grim – two wives with young children walked 140 miles almost alone through dense jungle, and were ultimately flown out by the Royal Dutch Air Force, but the majority of the European men remained at their posts, as they had done in Singapore. After some rough treatment from the Japanese on their arrival, they were interned in a compound of thatched huts outside the town, which grew steadily more dilapidated, while food became progressively worse and more scarce as time went on. P. C. V. Cobbold was murdered by the Japanese under tragic circumstances, as was also D. MacDonald, manager of the Sarawak Rubber Estates Limited.

The whole hideous episode not unnaturally left a lifelong mark on some members of the Company's staff. The most surprising thing, at least to the writer, is that today they do not feel more bitter about it than they do. Time is indeed a great healer.

In the meantime those at home were left almost completely without news of their relatives and colleagues for three and a half years. 'It is an extraordinary fact,' said the Chairman, Sir Adam Ritchie, in his annual speech to the shareholders in 1945, 'that an enemy, even as ruthless and efficient as the Japanese, should have been able to maintain this screen of secrecy for so long.' By the end of 1941 business was no longer going on as usual. It had ceased. The Chairman's report had shrunk to a small sheet of 'austerity' paper little larger than a postcard, stamped by the Ministry of Information Technical Censorship Division in red with 'Approved as not containing information of value to the enemy' and signed 'A. Fox'. In it he reported profits of £175,000 and tax of £155,000 – 'a crushing burden on companies with all their interests abroad where we are in competition with others who have not a similar burden to shoulder'. Soon there were to be no profits to tax at all.

By 1942 all the Company's property abroad was in enemy hands. In Siam everything, including the forest leases, was taken over by the Siamese. The following year was spent mostly in clearing up the incredible confusion from loss and diversion of cargoes and also in many cases all the documents. 'We are planning on the assumption,' the Chairman reported, 'that Siam will be the first country we shall be able to return to. I profess no more knowledge of allied strategy than anyone else but I think this is quite a fair bet.' In March of that year came the first glimmer of news, a broadcast message revealing that at least Martine and Scott were alive. In 1944 the total reckoning was: Captured, fifty-nine. Reported either as prisoners in war camps or interned as civilians, forty-eight. Missing or dead, seven. No news whatsoever, four.

Mention of the occupation of Singapore by the Japanese would not be complete without the names of Choy Khun Heng and his wife, Elizabeth. Mr Choy was a clerk in the accounts department of the Company's Singapore branch, and during the occupation he and his wife took over the tuck shop attached to the mental hospital in Yio Chu Kang Road, which the Japanese converted to a general hospital, for the use of the more seriously ill internees.

This enabled Mr and Mrs Choy to filter considerable supplies of provisions and money into Changi Gaol for the use of the sick. For this and other reasons the Choys were at length arrested by the Kempetai and were abominably tortured in front of one another. The pair had an agreement to say nothing, and they said nothing until advised otherwise by fellow prisoners. For their extraordinary fortitude and help to civilian internees, they were later decorated by the Government. Mrs Choy was received by the Queen, and later returned to London for Coronation celebrations in 1953.

Another member of the Company's staff, Lau Chai Lim, who was a salesman in Kuching, was the hero of an episode which deserves mention, partly because any act of daring and effrontery against the Japanese must be held meritorious and partly because it may well have saved much bloodshed among the liberation forces of the Allies. Mr Lau had spent most of the occupation period in hiding with his family. In 1945 when the Allied forces were approaching, Kuching was still occupied by Japanese troops and a battle for the town seemed certain. It was at this point that Mr Lau and his son smuggled themselves into the fort and ran up the Union Jack and the old flag of Sarawak. On seeing these the Japanese forces still in the town, believing themselves to be already surrounded, panicked and fled up-country. Kuching was liberated without bloodshed and for his great services to the community Mr Lau was appointed by the Rajah

*Before and after: the Bangkok office in 1939 and after its destruction by Allied bombs. It was used by the Japanese during the war as their transport headquarters*

to be an officer of the 'Most Excellent Order of the Star of Sarawak.'

A year before the war ended the Government at home were forming rehabilitation units to take over the various territories as they were liberated and in these the more senior members of the Borneo Company were to take a considerable part as being among the first civilians permitted to return. The diary of events in late 1945 shows the commendable urgency with which this business of commercial rehabilitation was put in hand. 15th August: Japan surrenders. 16th August: Siam cancels declaration of war. 16th September: Eastern general manager arrives in Bangkok as head of British Government mission for producing rice. 18th October: Bangkok office open for general business. 31st December: General manager, A. R. Malcolm, reaches Singapore. Early 1946: Company re-established in every pre-war sphere except in the Dutch East Indies.

It was possible at last to assess the losses, human and material. Eighteen members of the staff had lost their lives, either in fighting or as prisoners. So, it should be mentioned in gratitude, had a number of Malayan, Chinese, and Siamese sympathisers who had given surreptitious assistance and been caught and executed by the Japanese. In Bangkok the 'fine and imposing' office erected in 1925 had been battered to pieces, together with the surrounding wharves and warehouses, by Allied bombing. The manager's house had been wiped out but the sawmill seemed structurally sound. In Malaya and Sarawak material losses were considerable. In Kuching 'Aneberg', as the manager's bungalow has almost consistently been called since Helms so named the first one, after his wife, in the 1850s, had been used as a Japanese officers' brothel and was now a wreck. Losses of stock, furnishings, and plant were heavy, but as most of the records were lost it was impossible to make an accurate estimate. In Siam huge quantities of teak had been expropriated or stolen, though the peace treaty provided for restitution, Siam having emerged from the war as one of the richest countries in the East. It was decided that the Siamese agency which had been working the BCL teak concessions should continue for a further year under the supervision of the Company's staff. In Sarawak the rubber had overgrown and 'gone back' and so had many of the European owned plantations in Malaya, though from other estates it was possible even in 1946 to ship rubber in great quantities to Britain and the United States. Rehabilitation, helped by an efficient military set-up in Malaya, was quicker and more complete than most people had dared to hope. The political situation, however, was vague in the extreme and the whole of Malaya was littered with governors, high commissioners and other impressive-sounding functionaries of uncertain function. On the whole it was an uneasy time.

\*      \*      \*

One incident of deep concern to every long-standing member of the Company must now be mentioned, though it will not be for the present writer to make anything but impartial comment on it. On 24th September 1941, barely three months before the country was overrun, Sarawak had celebrated a hundred years of Brooke rule. Now, at the end of the war, the country was ceded to the Colonial Office by the third and last Rajah, HH Sir Charles Vyner Brooke, GCMG, who has been good enough to write a foreword to this book.

Life under Brooke rule would perhaps have been regarded as an anachronism today. Certainly this would be so in the eyes of the Government elected in Britain just after the war. Nevertheless it is indisputable that under Brooke rule the country had been a happy one. Different races had lived together in amicable harmony under benevolent autocracy that really did regard all of them as equal and respected their native customs. The Rajah's knowledge of native languages was probably unrivalled and even the humblest had direct access to him. It was not uncommon to see him pause on his way down to the Government offices in the morning and, with his topee pushed well back on his head and smoking a cigarette, hold informal converse with a Chinese rickshaw coolie in the bazaar. The young European arriving for the first time in Sarawak learnt very quickly that his nationality alone entitled him to no privileges or distinctions whatever. Perhaps the handing-over of Sarawak was, a natural and inevitable move with the times. Perhaps with the Rajah absent, by chance, in Australia, with all the Government officers interned by the Japanese and with much of the country's material assets pillaged and wrecked, the job of rehabilitation and in particular the financing thereof would have been too much for the Brookes and private enterprise. Suffice to say that after exactly a hundred years the partnership between benevolent autocratic rule in the person of the Rajahs and commercial enterprise in the shape of the Borneo Company, a partnership which had indisputably lifted Sarawak from primaeval

*The Company versus the forests of Sarawak; floating logs down the Rejang river*

savagery, had now come sadly to an end. It was a century on which both could look back with pride.

★     ★     ★

The period immediately after the war saw the most perfect seller's market in history. The territories to which the Company returned in the Far East had emerged from the war denuded of material goods but with a large amount of Government credit available through the banks. Anything could be sold – if only you could get hold of it to sell. Money was no object. Business was limited only by one's ability to secure material goods and by

*Kuching: 'Aneberg', home of BCL managers, is the white house on the hill*

*Chairman of The Borneo Company: C. R. Akers, FCA*

*A. R. Malcolm, managing director, whose
fifty-three years with the Company is a
record for length of service*

the measures taken by the British Government to try to divert as much as
possible to hard currency countries.

In Siam, 'the rice bowl of Asia', all exports of rice were meant to be
made through the International Merchandise Food Council and a large
proportion of the total legitimate export of rice was made through the Siam
Rice Agency in which British firms combined, with the Borneo Company
taking a prominent part. In the meantime gigantic fortunes were made by
Siamese, Chinese, and other non-European traders, who have never taken
kindly to orderly schemes, fixed prices, Government control, and the rest of
it, when millions of ticals or Straits dollars are to be picked up by evading
them.

In Malaya the road transport of the country was re-equipped by BCL
and their friendly rivals in the motor business, Wearne Brothers, acting in
temporary partnership. With all British Borneo now under Colonial Office
control the Company extended rapidly and was soon represented in every
town from Kuching to Sandakan. By 1949 the import business had more

*His Majesty King Bhumipol Adulyadet of Siam*

*Left, Talang Talang island, Sarawak; descendants-to-be of the turtles 'ridden' by Robert Henderson in 1874. Right, one of the five elephants from Chipperfield's Circus being slung ashore in Sarawak on arrival from England*

than trebled itself and the agency business was also flourishing as never before. Air travel was growing every day, especially in Bangkok, 'the Clapham Junction of the East', and the Company opened up, under the direction of a Siamese national of marked ability, an airways agency for bookings and passenger handling which has thrived consistently ever since.

Politics and the intrusion of governments formed the only cloud on the commercial horizon. Siam had by 1948 had eleven different Governments since the war. The new rulers of Indonesia stopped trade with Penang and Singapore, whereupon it was found that the Colonial Office at home, without apparent consultation with the Singapore or Federation Governments, acquiesced in the supply to Indonesia direct from Britain of goods which could more easily and more cheaply be supplied from Malaya. In that country Communist unrest was just beginning — in which connection more than one member of the Company who was a prisoner in Singapore makes

*Kuching: looking down river to the Company's headquarters*

the interesting speculation that a different post-war treatment of the Chinese and Malay guerillas who had harried the Japanese so persistently throughout the war might well have averted the whole of the present troubles there.

Apart from these man-made obstructions the sellers' market boomed solidly for four or five years. There had been times between the wars when companies like BCL, trading in the Far East and largely at the mercy of commodity prices, paid no dividend for years at a time and could concentrate only on keeping their heads above water till the coming of better days. Similarly when a wave of prosperity surged over the Far East after the war, those who were alert and possessed both the necessary connections and the know-how came in on the crest of it. In 1951 for the first time in its history the Borneo Company made a profit of over a million pounds – the liability for tax on which, it is painful to note, was the best part of six hundred

*HH the Sultan of Brunei, Sir Omar Ali Saifuddin Washadul Dhairi Waddin, KCMG, and his Consort at their coronation*

thousand. In the following year the turnover amounted to £16,000,000, the profit was £1,828,692 and the liability for tax was over £1,000,000. In 1953 the profit was still a million and a quarter but the wave was now showing signs of breaking. Rubber and tin prices were beginning to go down. Demands for new capital were constant. Nevertheless, it had undoubtedly been good while it lasted.

With the upsurge of nationalistic ambitions in Far Eastern countries after the war, it has become inevitable that the old 'exploitation' companies, using the word in its correct and better sense – companies like BCL who had either opened up virgin jungle, as in Borneo, or introduced western ideas of commerce, as in Siam – should give place, in the developing of natural resources, to the nationals of the countries concerned when the latter were anxious and able to take over, and very often when they weren't. A case in point is the teak which the Company has been extracting from the forests of northern Siam for the best part of a century. Nowadays the tendency is for the teak leases to be granted to Siamese nationals, and at the time of writing the future of this phase of the Company's activity in Siam is obscure. Like others of its kind it finds itself concentrating more and more on general trading of a kind which depends on strict attention to detail and comparatively small margins of profit.

In Sarawak the same conditions do not apply and the Company has come out of its corner to engage in a third round with the forest. Though one of two 'trial' elephants brought from Siam before the war had died, it was clear that the climate suited them perfectly well and that elephants were almost as indispensable in Sarawak as in Siam. Unfortunately, however, wartime losses had caused not only Siam but also India and Burma to prohibit their export. Looking nearer home, the Company turned to Chipperfield's Circus and bought five beasts aged eleven to seventeen years, at which age it was believed that they would remember nothing of their circus life when they reached the forest.

Advice having been taken from Elephant Bill, they were shipped on the upper deck of the P & O liner *Soudan*, together with rations including, among other things, 500 bales of hay, three cases of rum, and ten pounds of Epsom salts. Refreshed by 200 banana stems at Penang, they were transhipped at Singapore – after a good deal of trouble from one called Myrtle – and safely slung off at Sarikei fifty-two days after leaving Southampton. Their first action was to swim across the river, nearly half a mile

*Manhandling logs down to the Rejang river, Sarawak*

mile wide, and get bogged the other side. They were already, however, celebrated in their way, for during their journey they had been the subject of a
fourth leader in *The Times*. 'The mere fact that our export trade in elephants is in its infancy,' it said, 'does not deter the amateur economist from
pinning to it his hopes of national recovery.'

The elephants were duly set to work some ninety miles up the Rejang
where they carried out well enough their allotted tasks. The idea was to
float the logs down the Rejang, each hard one supported by a soft one on
either side. The rapids proved a formidable hazard and the sawmill, let it
be whispered, was once again in the wrong place. Even so the venture
might have prevailed, had not the bottom fallen out of the market and
finished it off. The elephants were sold to Chinese and the Company
retired to the Rejang delta, there to extract ramin wood from the swamps
through the medium of the Austral Timber Company. Ramin is a whitish

*Down in the forest: one of the elephants at work in Sarawak*

wood used a good deal for furniture and – touch wood indeed! – there is still a good market for it.

As to minerals in Sarawak the Company no longer holds the rights which it was given at the time of its birth but, so far as can be seen, Sarawak is a spent force in this direction. An expert prospector has recently completed two years on behalf of the Company, exploring the wilds of Upper Sarawak equipped with apparatus which Helms no doubt would have viewed with envy and delight, but the result has been a blank. Now, if anything is found, it will more likely be by the Royal Dutch Shell Company in their search for oil further up the coast. When oil was first discovered at Miri in 1910, the Borneo Company passed over its rights to Royal Dutch Shell in return for a marketing concession and on the understanding that any mineral deposits would be disclosed to the BCL.

\*     \*     \*

What a fantastic enterprise the Borneo Company of today would seem to the pioneers with whom this story began – Henderson, Harvey, the first Rajah, Helms, Adamson, Gilfillan, and the others – and how proud they would be if they could see it. They started with a capital of £60,000. Today, a hundred years later, the fixed and current assets are reckoned at £7,571,084, with twelve branch establishments in what is now British Borneo, five in Malaya and three in Siam. New offices in Kuching and Sibu await official opening by the Chairman, C. R. Akers, in the course of a tour which will take him to all these branches in celebration of the Centenary. He will be visiting an enterprise which, with its fifteen subsidiary companies, will sell you anything from a teak log to a box of matches, a barge to a bottle of beer; which will insure you, book you an air passage, victual your ships, or act as your agent whatever country you may live in and whatever you want to sell.

The secret of all these great 'venture' companies lies in flexibility, the way in which if one line of activity fails – as, for instance, the tea failed a couple of years ago in Sumatra, never having recovered from the war – they can immediately probe out elsewhere. And the secret of flexibility lies, of course, in human beings. This secret the Borneo Company has clearly possessed since its humblest beginnings. Soon after the turn of the century three men who had spent much of their lives in the Far East, Makepeace,

Brooke and Braddell, wrote a book, *A Hundred Years of Singapore*. In the course of it they pay to the Borneo Company a tribute which perhaps means more than any amount of facts, figures, balance sheets, and statistics.

'Of all companies,' they say, 'the Borneo Company has most had the knack of keeping its employees.'

In the London office and the East there are today no fewer than sixty people, British and Asiatic, who have spent more than twenty-five years of their life in the Company's service. In the course of its first hundred years three have served more than half a century. The first was Alexander Durward, who joined in 1866 and retired, as accountant to the London office, in 1919. The second was P. D. Thomson, who joined in 1868 and was managing director when he retired in 1918. The third, appropriately enough, is the present managing director, A. R. Malcolm, who joined in 1903, celebrated his fiftieth year of service by penetrating 400 miles up the Rejang river, and now holds the record with just over fifty-three years.

A little while ago three young fellows flew out to Bangkok, Singapore, and Kuching to start their careers with the Borneo Company. When someone in the year 2006 comes to write *The First 150 Years of the Borneo Company*, how splendid if he too can close his story by quoting their names!

# PEOPLE AND DATES

# MANAGING DIRECTORS GENERAL MANAGERS, MANAGERS,

### LONDON

| | | |
|---|---|---|
| William Martin | J. W. Edie | D. T. Lewis |
| John Harvey | O. M. Peiniger | A. R. Malcolm |
| Wm. Mulholland | A. A. Jamieson | Sir Adam Ritchie |
| P. D. Thomson | R. E. Henderson | K. H. Simpson |
| Andrew Currie | W. A. Akers | T. C. Martine |
| E. H. Finch | D. Robertson | I. L. MacEwen |
| | J. C. Ferrier | |

### *Secretaries*

| | | |
|---|---|---|
| A. Crawford | J. W. Edie | H. H. Gallie |
| J. Monro | O. M. Peiniger | E. Isitt |
| P. D. Thomson | R. V. Palmer | K. V. Smith |
| A. Currie | G. C. Durward | W. C. Lang |
| | E. A. Hudson | |

# MANAGERS, ETC, OF EASTERN BRANCHES, IN DATE SEQUENCE

### SARAWAK (BORNEO)

| | | |
|---|---|---|
| L. V. Helms | E. J. M. Smith | G. T. Bates |
| W. G. Brodie | C. D. Harvey | T. C. Martine |
| J. Hardie | J. M. Bryan | C. B. Horn |
| W. A. Cadell | C. Fenwick | |

### SINGAPORE (MALAYA)

| | | |
|---|---|---|
| John Harvey | C. Sugden | C. Jackson |
| Wm. Adamson | W. Patchitt | K. H. Simpson |
| P. W. Auchincloss | J. Denniston | N. J. Davies |
| Wm. Mulholland | D. T. Lewis | I. L. MacEwen |
| W. A. Cadell | F. E. Dilley | J. A. Donald |
| A. Currie | T. C. Martine | |

## BANGKOK (THAILAND)

S. Gilfillan
Wm. Adamson
John Gunn
P. W. Auchincloss
J. Blyth
H. Foss

F. S. Clarke
W. A. Cadell
C. S. Leckie
E. H. Finch
J. W. Edie
W. E. Adam
M. C. Cooke-Collis

A. R. Malcolm (GM)
G. A. C. Preston
K. H. Simpson
G. Watts
I. L. MacEwen
E. P. Heath

## CHIENGMAI (THAILAND)

L. T. Leonowens
C. S. Leckie

D. F. Macfie
R. W. S. Ogle
H. Lingard

A. R. Buchanan
R. W. Wood

## BATAVIA (DUTCH EAST INDIES)

John Black
P. W. Auchincloss
H. Duck

H. D. Jamieson
Wm. Lorrain
W. B. Ramage

J. C. Ferrier
A. W. G. Luke

## HONG KONG

H. Nicaise
J. Jamieson

E. Rose
H. Foss

W. G. Brodie

# CHAIRMEN OF DIRECTORS OF THE BORNEO COMPANY LIMITED

## 1856–1956

| | |
|---|---|
| Robert Henderson | 1856–71 |
| Francis Richardson | 1871–96 |
| George William Henderson | 1896–1925 |
| Sir Archibald A. Jamieson, MC | 1925–31 |
| Sir Adam B. Ritchie | 1931–50 |
| C. R. Akers | 1950– |

# DIRECTORS OF THE BORNEO COMPANY LIMITED

## 1856–1956

| | |
|---|---|
| Robert Henderson | 1856–71 |
| John C. Templer | 1856–74 |
| J. Dyce Nicol, MP | 1856–69 |
| John Smith | 1856–68 |
| Francis Richardson | 1856–96 |
| John Harvey | 1859–79 |
| George Henderson | 1863–85 |
| William Martin | 1874–90 |
| Robert Henderson (II) | 1876–95 |
| George Henderson (II) | 1885–1906 |
| Albert Harvey | 1885–1912 |
| P. D. Thomson | 1890–1916 |
| John Henderson | 1895–1922 |
| Geo. Wm. Henderson | 1895–1931 |
| R. Evelyn Henderson | 1910–25 |
| Col. John Harvey, DSO | 1910–22 |
| E. C. Grenfell, MP (Lord St Just) | 1916–22 |
| Sir Archibald A. Jamieson, MC | 1921–37 |
| Arthur Whitworth | 1921–46 |
| H. A. Trotter | 1923–41 |
| J. K. Henderson | 1926–54 |
| Sir Adam B. Ritchie | 1930–54 |
| J. W. Hely-Hutchinson | 1937–50 |
| D. T. Lewis | 1941–55 |
| A. R. Malcolm | 1946– |
| C. R. Akers | 1949– |
| K. H. Simpson | 1950– |
| R. A. Henderson | 1954– |
| J. R. Grey | 1954– |
| I. L. MacEwen | 1955– |

# ROLL OF HONOUR

### SARAWAK REBELLION

| | | |
|---|---|---|
| 1857 | R. WELLINGTON | *Killed whilst trying to protect the women and children* |

### SINGAPORE MUTINY

| | | |
|---|---|---|
| 1915 | A. H. EVANS | *Killed by mutineers* |

### KEDAH, MALAYA

| | | |
|---|---|---|
| 1922 | J. DOUGHTY SMITH | *Killed by dacoit* |

### PAKNAMPHO, SIAM, FIRE

| | | |
|---|---|---|
| 1924 | A. D. ELLISON | *Died from injuries suffered whilst trying to rescue Company's books* |

### 1914–1918 WAR

## KILLED IN ACTION

T. B. CHATTERIS (SIAM) — Capt, Sherwood Foresters
A. M. DUNN (LONDON) — Sergt, Honorable Artillery Company
D. F. FERGUSON (LONDON) — Capt, Scottish Horse
J. G. GOFFEY (LONDON) — 2/Lieut, Kings Royal Rifle Corps
F. HILTON (SINGAPORE) — Major, Singapore Volunteer Artillery (Drowned through enemy action)

G. S. LEWIS (LONDON) — Capt, Middlesex Regiment
J. O. McCAROGHER (LONDON) — Pte, London Scottish
L. F. STEVENS (LONDON) — 2/Lieut, East Surrey Regiment
S. N. WADDY (LONDON) — 2/Lieut, Royal Air Force
L. D. WICKHAM (LONDON) — Capt, Lincolnshire Regiment

### WORLD WAR, 1939–1945

## KILLED IN ACTION

G. C. ASHWORTH (MALAYA) — Lt Com, MRNVR — *Killed in action, Banka Straits, ss Scorpion*

O. BELLINGHAM-SMITH (MALAYA) — Capt, FMSVR — *Died, prisoner of war, Thailand*

| | | |
|---|---|---|
| G. BROCKMANN (MALAYA) | Lieut, MVF | *Died, prisoner of war, Thailand* |
| W. CASSELS (SUMATRA) | POW, Malaya | *Killed when ship torpedoed* |
| P. C. V. COBBOLD (SARAWAK) | POW, Sarawak | *Killed by Japanese in Borneo* |
| C. V. CROWTHER-SMITH (MALAYA) | Lieut, MVF | *Died of wounds in action in Singapore before capitulation* |
| E. F. ECKFORD (MALAYA) | Sergt, SSVF | *Died, prisoner of war, Borneo* |
| E. S. ENNALS (SIAM) | 2/Lieut, Punjab Regiment | *Killed in action, Syria* |
| J. E. HARVEY (MALAYA) | Pte, SSVF | *Died, prisoner of war, Changi, Singapore* |
| E. C. HAYWOOD (MALAYA) | Lieut, MVF | *Killed in action, Malaya* |
| T. P. JONES (MALAYA) | Lieut, Malay Regiment | *Died, prisoner of war, Thailand* |
| J. A. LAIDLAW (MALAYA) | Lieut, SSVF | *Drowned when Japanese transport sunk* |
| H. G. LEVINE (LONDON) | Pte, RAPC | *Killed in air raid, London* |
| D. MACDONALD (SARAWAK) | POW, Sarawak | *Killed by Japanese in Borneo* |
| R. G. MAUND (MALAYA) | F/O, RAF | *Died, prisoner of war, Malaya* |
| R. L. MOIR (MALAYA) | Pte, MVF | *Died, prisoner of war, Thailand* |
| W. R. RAVIE (MALAYA) | Sergt, Australian Infantry | *Killed in action, New Guinea* |
| J. E. SLADE (MALAYA) | F/Lieut, RAF | *Killed in action, English Channel* |
| L. SMITH (LONDON) | | *Killed in air raid, London* |
| K. A. VAN DEN BERG (SUMATRA) | POW | *Died, Burma* |
| K. S. WALKER (MALAYA) | F/O, RAFVR | *Died in England on release, prisoner of war, Sumatra* |

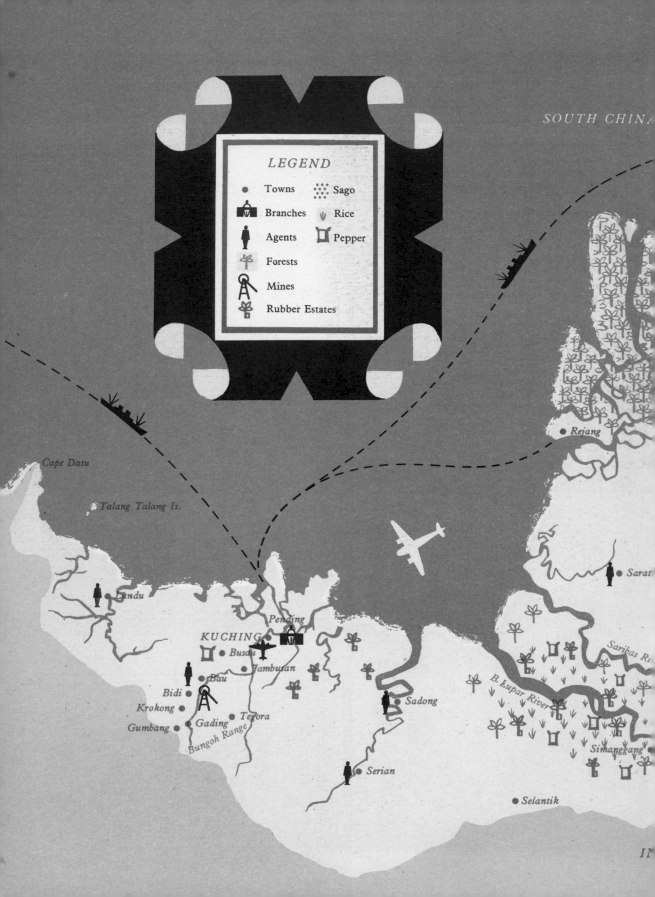

SOUTH CHINA

**LEGEND**

- Towns
- Branches
- Agents
- Forests
- Mines
- Rubber Estates

∴ Sago
🌾 Rice
⊡ Pepper

Cape Datu

Talang Talang Is.

Rejang

Sarat

Lundu

Pending

KUCHING

Busau

Jambusan

Bau

Bidi

Krokong

Gading    Tegora

Gumbang

Bungoh Range

Sadong

B. Lupar River

Saribas R.

Serian

Selantik

Simanggang

IN